Facilitating Educational Success for Migrant Farmworker Students in the U.S.

Grounded in empirical research, this timely volume examines the challenges to academic success that migrant farmworker students face in the U.S. Providing an original framework for academic success among migrant farmworker students and applying a diverse range of methodological approaches, chapter authors address a range of topics, including English Language Learner development; support for educators who work with migrant farmworker students; promotion of migrant family involvement; and college access. This book provides pragmatic strategies and interventions and considers practical and policy implications to increase migrant student academic achievement and support migrant farmworker students and families.

Patricia A. Pérez is Professor of Chicana/o Studies at California State University, Fullerton, USA.

Maria Estela Zarate is Professor of Educational Leadership at California State University, Fullerton, USA.

Routledge Research in Educational Equality and Diversity

For a full list of titles in this series, please visit www.routledge.com

Books in the series include:

Youth in Education
The Necessity of Valuing Ethnocultural Diversity
Christiane Timmerman, Noel Clycq, Marie McAndrew, Alhassane Balde, Luc Braekmans, Sara Mels

Identity, Neoliberalism and Aspiration
Educating White Working-class Boys
Garth Stahl

Faces of Discrimination in Higher Education in India
Quota Policy, Social Justice and the Dalits
Samson K. Ovichegan

Inequality, Power and School Success
Case Studies on Racial Disparity and Opportunity in Education
Gilberto Q. Conchas and Michael A. Gottfried with Briana M. Hinga

Youth & Inequality in Education
Global Actions in Youth Work
Dana Fusco and Michael Heathfield

Social Justice and Transformative Learning
Culture and Identity in the United States and South Africa
Edited by Saundra M. Tomlinson-Clarke and Darren L. Clarke

Race and Colorism in Education
Edited by Carla R. Monroe

Facilitating Educational Success for Migrant Farmworker Students in the U.S.
Edited by Patricia A. Pérez and Maria Estela Zarate

Facilitating Educational Success for Migrant Farmworker Students in the U.S.

Edited by
Patricia A. Pérez and
Maria Estela Zarate

NEW YORK AND LONDON

First published 2017
by Routledge
711 Third Avenue, New York, NY 10017

and by Routledge
2 Park Square, Milton Park, Abingdon, Oxon, OX14 4RN

Routledge is an imprint of the Taylor & Francis Group, an informa business

© 2017 Taylor & Francis

The right of Patricia A. Pérez and Maria Estela Zarate to be identified as editors of this work has been asserted by them in accordance with sections 77 and 78 of the Copyright, Designs and Patents Act 1988.

All rights reserved. No part of this book may be reprinted or reproduced or utilised in any form or by any electronic, mechanical, or other means, now known or hereafter invented, including photocopying and recording, or in any information storage or retrieval system, without permission in writing from the publishers.

Trademark notice: Product or corporate names may be trademarks or registered trademarks, and are used only for identification and explanation without intent to infringe.

Library of Congress Cataloguing-in-Publication Data
A catalog record for this book has been requested.

ISBN: 978-1-138-22016-4 (hbk)
ISBN: 978-1-315-41381-5 (ebk)

Typeset in Sabon
by Apex CoVantage, LLC

To Diego, great-grandson of former *bracero* Jesus Zarate Robledo

To Matías and Andrés, great-grandsons of former *bracero* José Merced Pineda García

Contents

Preface	ix
Foreword	xv
JUAN FELIPE HERRERA	
Acknowledgements	xix

1 **Migrant Education: Equity in Context for Farmworkers and Their Children**   1
MARIA ESTELA ZARATE, PATRICIA A. PÉREZ, AND RODOLFO ACOSTA

2 **Educational Initiatives Supporting Students from Migrant Farmworker Backgrounds**   14
ANN CRANSTON-GINGRAS AND GEORGINA RIVERA-SINGLETARY

3 **Helping Educators Connect with Migrant Students and Families: A Culturally Proficient Approach**   32
REYES L. QUEZADA, FERNANDO RODRÍGUEZ-VALLS, AND RANDALL B. LINDSEY

4 ***Nuestra Familia es Nuestra Fuerza*: Building on the Strengths of Migrant Families Towards School Success**   50
PABLO JASIS AND ALEJANDRO GONZÁLEZ

5 **Designing Programs to Meet and Assess the Needs of Migrant Students**   67
FERNANDO RODRÍGUEZ-VALLS AND SANDRA KOFFORD

6 **What Can Latina/o Migrant Students Tell Us about College Outreach and Access?**   82
ANNE-MARIE NÚÑEZ

viii   *Contents*

7 Migrant Education and Shifting Consciousness: A Cultural
   Wealth Approach to Navigating Politics, Access, and Equity   94
   CRISTINA ALFARO, KAREN CADIERO-KAPLAN, AND SERA HERNANDEZ

8 From the Fields to Fieldwork: *Cuentos* from the Daughter
   of Migrant Farmworkers   113
   EBELIA HERNÁNDEZ

9 Conclusion: Future Directions for Migrant Education   121
   PATRICIA A. PÉREZ AND MARIA ESTELA ZARATE

   List of Acronyms   127
   List of Contributors   129
   Index   133

Preface

Human progress and intellectual growth can be attributed, in part, to centuries of human migration. For centuries, kingdoms, nations, and conquerors have relied on migrant labor to build infrastructure and feed the people. The nationalities or regional origins of migrant workers and the land owners change over time, but the role of the migrant worker in society remains the same: critical to the survival of the people and yet a shadow in the sidelines in our social and political stage. Today, migrant farmworkers hail from developing countries to the U.S. and western Europe. Much like in the U.S., migrant farmworkers in western Europe arrive from poorer neighboring countries. Bulgarians pick stone fruit in eastern Turkey, Romanians pick vegetables in southern Italy, and poorer neighbors from the Baltic states pick strawberries in Sweden. Like those in the U.S., migrant workers around the world are unseen by consumers.

Occasionally visible to travelers, migrant farmworkers are seen in overcrowded beds of pick-up trucks along rural roads, small figures bent over in immense fields with endless rows of harvest, and arriving to border checkpoints and urban ports with modest bundles of belongings. In other regions, migrant farmworkers are fellow countrymen who have been excluded from national economic progress. In countries such as Mexico, India, and China, migrant farmworkers are members of indigenous groups, marginalized castes, and rural citizens left behind from urbanization ambitions.

Regardless of origins, migrant farmworkers are recognizable by weathered faces, darker phenotypes, and worn, calloused hands. In the social order of labor work, farm work is one of the harshest and least desirable occupations where workers are exposed to nature's extreme temperaments. The children of farmworkers are also burdened by the itinerant lifestyle, unstable income, frequent residential relocation, and the feelings of alienation of being "new" or a "stranger" to new schools. Farmworker families often traverse large geographic expanses with their children cradled on their backs or picking alongside their parents. Understandably, migrant farmworker parents hope and dream that their children move on to less severe occupations. And in some contexts, children of farmworkers are able to exit farm work onto more desirable occupational trajectories. One such storyline

x   *Preface*

is the inspiration, in part, to this volume. Dr. Pérez's own familiar history is one such illustration of how a farmworker family began their journey in native lands to pursue foreign soil in this abstract pursuit of the American Dream. Indeed, José Merced Pineda García's story continues to inspire her support of migrant farmworker students, families, and communities.

Patricia's Family History

Like many other migrant farmworkers in the U.S., José Merced Pineda García's story began in Mexico. More specifically, my maternal grandfather was born on a ranch in Valencianita, near Irapuato, Guanajuato. In the 1950s, he moved his family from Arizona to the agricultural town of Santa Paula, California. As it did for other male immigrants of his generation, the *Bracero* Program, a guest worker program between the U.S. and Mexico, allowed him to work in the U.S. legally for six months at a time. He was known as No. 705812. His destination was not a calculated move. Instead, he and his cousin arrived to the registration site in Mexico City, noticed the line to work in California was longer than the Arizona line, and so they registered to participate in Arizona. Little did he know, there was a reason why the Arizona line was much shorter. Unlike others, he and his cousin did not have to wait long to begin work because he knew how to drive a tractor— a skill that made him stand out relative to other migrant farmworkers. And so he and his cousin started working for the Arizona Cotton Growers Association in Phoenix, Arizona. That was the first time my grandfather had come to this country legally. Understandably, Arizona was an awful place to work in the fields. It was hot and dry, and he performed extremely laborious work. In fact, his cousin ended up passing out one day working in the fields and returned to Mexico. Undeterred, José Merced Pineda García would continue working in Arizona alone.

Prior to this experience, my grandfather had worked illegally in the fields, moving throughout California and Texas, even doing a stint in Santa Paula. After his first child was born, he and my grandmother decided to move to Santa Paula in the 1950s. They were attracted to Santa Paula because there was steady work; that is, my grandfather would not have to migrate searching for work, and there were good schools. Like many other migrant farmworker families, education was always important to my grandfather, so access to good schools was key.

My grandfather worked for the *Limoneira* company in Santa Paula, where the weather was much, much better relative to the Arizona climate. He started as a "picker" on April 8, 1955, working in the orchards, and eventually making his way up until retiring, on December 31, 1996, as a "fruit receiver," transferring pallets of fruit with his heavy machinery. He had worked for the *Limoneira* company for over 40 years. His name is among those listed and honored on the Santa Paula Farmworkers Monument on 9th and Santa Barbara Streets, not too far from Dolores Huerta and Cesar Chavez's names, long-time farmworker union activists who co-founded the UFW, or United Farm Workers, along with Larry Itliong.

From the onset, my grandparents and my parents ingrained in my siblings and I a tremendous hard-work ethic that we would translate into the education setting. They knew education would open doors and they wanted us to better ourselves and take advantage of the opportunities available to us through education. More importantly, they made sacrifices on our behalf. As such, the scholar activism (or the "work") that I engage in is a direct result of the way I choose to honor the sacrifices that my ancestors, grandparents, and parents have made.

Educational access was a pivotal role in my history. Indeed, how students are accommodated and integrated into schools and educational systems has important implications for the long-term outcomes of farmworkers' children and grandchildren. Because children of farmworkers are marginalized in most contexts, it becomes important to focus on the unique challenges and assets of farmworker families to build educational policy and programs to support them. We offer this volume as a resource to highlight progressive and pragmatic strategies that can augment the educational opportunities of migrant children.

Comprehensive Needs Assessment Epiphany

Another important motivation for this book is derived from our recent work as co-principal investigators on a comprehensive needs assessment for a local Migrant Education Program (MEP). In carrying out the needs assessment, we were struck by the lack of a centralized and comprehensive body of research that would aid MEP staff and educators in supporting the academic success of migrant students along the PK-20 spectrum. Our most important goal in completing this text was to contribute to the dearth of research on best practices and programming aimed at supporting migrant farmworker students.

In an effort to contribute to the limited research on migrant farmworker students in the U.S., we set out to complete a volume that addressed this critical research from a multi-disciplinary and methodological approach. We brought together leading scholar-practitioners, all with very personal connections to migrant farmworker communities, to propel research that supports the educational advancement of migrant students noticeably forward. We hope to increase awareness and visibility regarding migrant education and migrant students in a U.S. context. Further, the chapter authors engage in various theories and methodological approaches to broach research on migrant farmworker students, as most are well aware that there is no such thing as a "one size fits all" approach when it comes to students. Finally, our aim is to provide educators and personnel working with migrant populations practical tools and strategies to facilitate their educational success.

xii *Preface*

Organization of the Book

Juan Felipe Herrera, U.S. poet laureate and the son of migrant farmworkers, opens the volume with his moving story of his father's migration to the U.S. and shares the critical role of words, songs, *dichos*, education, language, and caring educators. Ultimately, Herrera reminds us that it is important to use our voices as catalysts for change. In the introductory chapter, Zarate, Pérez, and Acosta provide a brief overview of the policy climate and ongoing research in migrant education. The authors address the role of educational policy as well as the development of migrant farmworker populations via U.S. transnational and economic trends. Subsequently, Cranston-Gingras and Rivera-Singletary share major education initiatives that have been developed to support migrant farmworker students and families. Further, they give particular attention to migrant students with disabilities, as well as students with English Language Learner backgrounds.

Next, Quezada, Rodríguez-Valls, and Lindsey describe their model of cultural proficiency and argue that only through inclusive practices and self-reflection can educators truly create equitable education practices for migrant students and families. Subsequently, the following chapter, authored by Jasis and González, employs the lens of empowerment theory to highlight how migrant parents describe and engage in leadership and advocacy on behalf of their children and their education. Astutely, the authors offer voices from migrant farmworker parents who are often rendered invisible and marked as "not involved" or "not interested" in their children's schooling. In "Designing Programs to Meet and Assess the Needs of Migrant Students," authors Rodríguez-Valls and Kofford use an asset-based framework to draw from migrant students' "funds of knowledge" to describe an applicable culturally and linguistically responsive assessment methodology that can guide sound and relevant program-building.

In Chapter Six, Núñez introduces the Multilevel Model of Intersectionality that reveals micro-, meso-, and macro-level factors that impede migrant student educational opportunity and college access. Included are an analysis of and perspectives from students who participated in the Migrant Student Leadership Institute. Using a cultural wealth approach, Alfaro, Cadiero-Kaplan, and Hernandez outline how key federal and state migrant education policies are framed and the extent to which students, educators, and community members are involved. Furthermore, the authors argue that researchers should "focus on and learn from the array of existent cultural knowledge, skills, abilities, and contacts possessed by migrant communities, that often go unrecognized and unacknowledged." Chapter Eight, authored by Hernández, draws from her experiences as the daughter of migrant farmworkers to discuss her educational journey from the almond fields to academic fieldwork. Each of the aforementioned chapters offers practical implications and guidance for programming, practices, and/or policy that, woven together, holistically support the migrant family unit. The final chapter, by Pérez and Zarate, provides an overview of the "lessons learned" throughout the volume and offers future directions for migrant education at the local, state, and federal levels.

While this volume only begins to cover the range of programs and services necessary, and the research needed to support migrant farmworker students and families in the U.S., we hope that this text serves as a critical resource for educators, researchers, policymakers, personnel, and/or organizations who are in need of empirical and evidence-based data to drive progress and reform. It is only through awareness and visibility that we can conceive, improve, and provide better educational opportunities for migrant farmworker students and families. As a nation built on the contributions of immigrants and migrants, we can and must do better.

Foreword

Juan Felipe Herrera

Voice Lessons

After jumping a train from Chihuahua at 14, my father, Felipe Emilio, crossed into Denver about 1889—for a penny each, there he purchased words in English (from his campesino-working-in-the-snow friends). My mother, Lucha, learned songs—in an "asilo"—an orphanage in Mexico City. "We were so poor," she would say, "mamá left me for a year." Later, in 1918, another train roared towards El Norte, to Júarez—this time, carrying my mother, grandmother, Juanita, and aunt Aurelia. Soon, they crossed that thin line of power into El Paso, Texas. The questions of power and culture would be the key to all things, soon enough.

Mamá enrolled into school hungry for letters, books, and the life of the learned—until third grade. "Since you seem to like stealing candy and hanging out with your friends more than going to 'la escuela,' I am pulling you out. And since you are the youngest, you will remain with me until the day that I die." Mamá Lucha persevered. She taught herself. She listened to radio words, radio stories, and radio dramas—most of all phrases intertwined with music, melody, and deep feeling—monologues and songs. Words for a penny in the ice of the Southwest for a man ready to conquer the North Country and songs from the last rung of social existence for a girl at the beginning of the twentieth century in the U.S.—this was my inheritance. This was my first set of voice lessons in my personal journey for an authentic self, a blue-print as a speaker, and later, a poet for the people. It began with the rhymes my mother learned in the orphanage of the poorest of the poor.

Words, rhymes, songs, *dichos*, and *adivinanzas* and my own clowny dramas in my father's hand-made campesino trailer that he built on top of a found car were my beginner's tool-kit, my "How to Become a Poet" map. Every day my mother recited, sang, danced, performed every verbal art that she could remember and patch together and little by little prepared me for my life as a speaker and poet. Every day I repeated her various arts, improvised, sang along, and added my own creations and style. This Mexico City and campesino "home-schooling" was thick with literary treasures, dreamy descriptions of the early 1900s in the post-war capitol and turn-of-the-century presidents, Porfirio Díaz and Francisco I. Madero. All this I carried with me

xvi *Juan Felipe Herrera*

when I opened the green painted door at Central Elementary in Escondido, California. After 10 seconds in class, I was spanked for not knowing English—from then on, I was silent, afraid, and ashamed—until a miracle took place in Barrio Logan Heights, San Diego—Lowell Elementary, in third grade.

"Sing a song." Mrs. Lelya Sampson said inviting me to the front of class. Her voice was tender, it was patient—I could feel her warmth and care covering me like a zarape. After I sang "Three Blind Mice" in front of my first audience in 1956, Mrs. Sampson offered me five magic words that changed my life. "You have a beautiful voice." "My voice?" "Beautiful?" At the end of the year, I sang a solo for our choir's "Swing Low Sweet Chariot" Gospel piece. Standing up, white shirt, Levis, and scuffed shoes—I looked out into the school's end-of-the-year, full attendance assembly and cast my voice out its full, open-petals. "Is this what a beautiful voice can do?" I said. Then we moved far, far away.

In San Francisco's Mission District, my cousin Vicente and I delivered tortillas for my uncle Beto's Mexica-tessen, cooked by his own original, self-designed, and incredible tortilla machine. A few blocks away, at the Mission Branch Boys Club on Alabama Street, I slipped on baggy boxing gloves at the behest of my all-knowing cousin Vicente—and battled the ruffians—and lost in the first 10 seconds of my amazing debut as the tallest dude in the history of the fourth grade team. There was another team that called me: the jazzy notes my cousin Tito played on his "Beatnik" phonograph—his Brubeck piano specials, his Thelonius Monk vinyls, and most of all, his Afro-Cuban Mongo Santamaría albums with Cal Trader at the lead tapping his mellifluous xylophone. Jazz and Cuba, Afro-rhythms and the trance-like atmosphere took me by surprise. The surprise was thick as the art of the times. In the basement, my older cousin, Beto, hung Calder-like "mobiles" from the ceiling and painted, with Tito, red eyes on the indigo-splashed walls. My mind was electric, my imagination, made of a thousand rhymes and stories. One thing was missing: my voice. It had retreated—until much later when we moved back to San Diego. At Roosevelt Junior High, Mr. Shuster abruptly stopped his lesson on Beethoven and asked me an impossible question that no one had ever asked anyone.

"What are you?" Mr. Shuster said. Maybe it was my silence that irked him. Maybe I was like the "H Man" at the movies, a weird atomic mutation. "Hawaiian." I said. "Mexican" was an im-poss-ible word. A word from another planet. A planet from the underground where my father picked grapes and my mother washed dishes for the rich. This was the second volley of words that changed my life. For the worse—I thought. But, these words charged my 7th grade mind. "From now on, I am not going to lie," I said to myself. "From this day forward, I am not going to be ashamed." As of this fall, when school starts I am going to dive into the fire. And I will rise up a new furry human being with a velvet voice—more handsome than Jerry Lewis and more powerful than "Super Boy." *I will be me.* So, I crossed an X

Foreword   xvii

on the registration card for the class that I hated. And bit my tongue for the whole summer. On the first day of class, I walked into the new experiment—Dr. Rossi's weird and nervous classroom.

"Please step forward, Juan. Closer. Listen to Mark's piano phrasing. Got it?" Silence. I was alone with the tenors behind me, the sopranos and altos to my right, and basses and baritones to my left. Looked down at my feet and noticed that they were tiptoeing at the edge of the world. Ahead, there were boy-eating double-headed sharks. Dove in—sang and sang and sang for years. Until I was a senior. By then I had been on stage. Barber Shop quartets and Madrigals. Gospels and Christmas assemblies. Tours to colleges and presentations of the choir in English and Spanish—little by little my wounded sparrow voice was coming alive. Five years in choir, every day—a little louder until somewhere in that trembling tiny voice there was a boy with a song at last. Before I knew it senior year was over and ahead of me was something much more miraculous, daring, and terrible that no one ever imagined, bigger than me, colossal—something that was about to explode and change the entire globe, like a tidal wave churned by twisting voices of the entire planet. I had no choice in this matter. A letter urged me—it was an EOP Grant to UCLA. Alurista lent me his father's suitcase and my own—a cardboard box tied with a rope and all the clothes I could pack. "Adios, adios," waved my mother at 1482 "B" Street across the street from Bradley's Hamburgers, downtown San Diego. "Adios mama," I said.

The Wilshire bus dropped me off at the gates of UCLA—and at the gates of the Chican@ Movimiento. Of course, no one knew that yet. I took in all the new sounds, rhythms, and words, styles, and beats on campus—Charles Lloyd Quartet jazz concerts, Jimi Hendrix fresh from London, Reis Lopez "El Tigre" Tijerina at the Grand Ballroom, Luis Valdez fresh from Cuba, the James Cotton Blues Band, and the Rudy Perez Modern Dance Ballet from New York. It was a multi-colored and a freestyle stage of open-ended experiments that pushed me further—all the way to the Free Speech mound in Kerkhoff Plaza where I trembled and squeaked like Mickey Mouse facing a few students eating organic cereal. At the mic, I noticed that I had a ways to go. Noticing Black poets improvising poems with phonographs playing, I took on Jazz poetry—added modern dance, color slides. What else could be done? In 1968, after seeing "No Le Saco Nada a La Escuela" by El Teatro Campesino in San Francisco's Dolores Park, a few blocks from my mother's apartment on Mission and 16th, I decided that I had to form my own teatro Chicano. Something bigger than me fueled me. It came from the streets. It came from Police chasing me along with the students that had just jumped their high school fences in East LA—the High School Blowouts. The fuel was called Purpose, it was called Change, and it was called Love.

The fuel also was channeled by my own circle of like-minded, first-generation campus rebels—UMAS (United Mexican-American Students) which morphed into MEChA. Our agenda went from affirmative action demands on campus to national and international calls to end the war in Viet Nam. Change, xviii *Juan Felipe Herrera*

War—Peace, and Culture were my Majors. Everyone was talking about Cultura. "Talk is cheap," I said. Let's meet it face to face.

After receiving a grant from the brand-new Chicano Research Center in 1970, with a crew of friends from class, I chose to go to the Lacandón Rain Forests of Najá and Lacanjá Chan Sayab in Chiapas. "There are only 500 Lacandón Mayas left in the last burnt rain forests," I told them. A people, a culture in danger—"This is what my voice is for—to save lives," I said to myself. There was a paradox waiting for me in the southernmost region of Mexico.

In the plaza of San Cristobal de Las Casas across from the El Jardín Hotel, reading the Excelsior newspaper, I stopped breathing, for a moment: "Youths Killed in Demonstrations at the Chicano Moratorium against the Viet Nam War, East LA—August 29, 1970." El Norte was just as endangered as the South. Indígena languages, communities shooed into the realms of malaria and starvation were on a par with Chican@ neighborhoods and schools and culture being denied and Latin@ youth lured into troubled wars. The trouble was also present in the jungles, mountains, and coasts of Mexico where we filmed, interviewed, and photographed the True Peoples, Hach Winik, as the Lacandondes would say. In the mountains of Nayarit, in Huichol Country, the squalor was the same, the encroachment of the Ladinos, Mexican Nationals, was the same, and in Papantla and Tuxpam, Veracruz, on Totonac lands, similar conditions existed. Existence, the lives of the peoples, their culture, voices, and stories—that "cultura" that we "celebrated" in El Norte—I had met it head on. They would remain endangered, cut-off from society and from fertile inquiry of the Chican@ Movement if I did not present all this back in the States. It was time to head back to the starting point.

On the trek back to El Norte, in a friend's green VW van, idling at Mexicali's border checkpoint with recordings, photographs, yarn paintings, gourds, and 10,000 feet of 16mm film—I realized I was helpless. The project to assist in changing the life conditions of "my people" swept into regions of danger was bigger than me. It was impossible. Maybe I was just talking to myself—people were busy with economic mobility and careers for themselves. Just one thing was possible—to change my self, to cast my voice.

Juan Felipe Herrera, U.S. Poet Laureate
July 19, 2016

Acknowledgements

We would like to thank the Migrant Education Program Region IX staff and Director Monica Nava for allowing us to continue to engage with the migrant farmworker community. We are also grateful to our amazing volume contributors who are committed to the educational success of migrant students and families. Finally, we are especially humbled to have Juan Felipe Herrera's words to initiate the conversation in this volume.

Chapter 3, "Helping Educators Connect with Migrant Students and Families: A Culturally Proficient Approach," is a summary of *Teaching and Supporting Migrant Children in Our Schools: A Culturally Proficient Approach* (New York, NY: Rowman & Littlefield Publishers, 2016). Grateful acknowledgement is made to Rowman & Littlefield Publishers for permission to publish this content.

1 Migrant Education
Equity in Context for Farmworkers and Their Children

Maria Estela Zarate, Patricia A. Pérez, and Rodolfo Acosta

According to the Office of Migrant Education, there are over 850,000 migrant[1] students identified in the U.S., the vast majority of whom are of Latino descent. Based on the most recent data available (2012–2013) through the U.S. Department of Education (2016), over 360,000 students are eligible to participate in Migrant Education Program (MEP) services based on three-year mobility criteria. Unfortunately, migrant farmworker children are among the most educationally disadvantaged groups in the U.S. (Gándara & Contreras, 2010). Despite the growing educational research on migrant farmworker students in the U.S., a comprehensive body of research providing pragmatic strategies for academic success among migrant farmworker students has yet to emerge. Grounded in empirical and evidence-based research, this timely edited volume seeks to address this gap in the literature by introducing different approaches to facilitating academic success for migrant farmworker students. Major topics addressed in this edited volume include fostering English Language Learner development, supporting educators and staff who work with migrant students and families, promoting familial involvement, increasing preparation for college, and identifying migrant student and family resources. More importantly, this text offers pragmatic intervention strategies, and practical and policy implications to increase migrant student academic achievement. This distinct body of work will be of interest to educators, policymakers, and personnel working with migrant students and families within the U.S. educational system. This volume will also be of interest to educators in an international context who work to promote educational success for migratory populations around the world.

This chapter provides an overview of the research available on migrant education. First, the chapter provides key policy goals and an overview of the MEP population, highlighting characteristics and trends that present challenges to their educational trajectory, including socioeconomic status, English Language Learner status, school attainment, educational achievement, and health indicators. Second, in addressing current challenges, the authors underscore various shifts in education and economic policy that have had implications for MEP participants, including students and their families.

2 Maria Estela Zarate et al.

Migrant Education in the Context of National Policy

The original conceptualization of the Elementary and Secondary Education Act (ESEA), the legislative act that allocated funding to MEP, advanced an equity agenda. The language driving ESEA focused on providing access to high quality schools regardless of income (Goodlad & Keating, 1990). More specifically, ESEA provided students with high quality supplemental programs intended to make up for perceived cultural and actual economic disadvantages (Acosta, Burch, Good, & Stewart, 2013). The theory of action behind MEP, as envisioned through an equity lens undergirding broader federal policy, is to provide resources for State Educational Agencies (SEA) to implement high quality and comprehensive supplemental educational programs for migratory children. The scope of these programs is aimed at mitigating the impact of educational outcomes they may suffer based on the high mobility of this population. Key elements within MEP also focus on providing state agencies with the resources necessary to design programs that would appropriately address challenges faced by migrant students. In other words, MEP services are aimed at bridging achievement gaps that may result from the high rate of student mobility. In addition to high residential mobility among migrant families, other unique challenges often faced by migrant farmworker students include being classified with limited English proficiency, social and cultural isolation, perceived family disengagement, poverty, fear of deportation, lack of student schooling, lack of qualified staff, outside political forces, and mobility (Arzubiaga, Noguerón, & Sullivan, 2009; McDonnell & Hill, 1993).

The most recent reauthorization of ESEA, known as the Every Student Succeeds Act (ESSA), further prioritizes support for SEAs. Different from NCLB, which designed student performance targets, school ratings, and support for struggling schools at the federal level, ESSA pushed for states to design and develop the various accountability metrics to measure school and student achievement. Although the federal government provided SEAs with more flexibility to design their accountability systems, similar to NCLB, states and LEAs have to provide disaggregated data on specific student subgroups, including migrant status. More so, ESSA requires states to describe how they and their LEAs are using federal and other funds to close achievement gaps and provide all students equitable access to a high-quality education, including program-specific requirements necessary to ensure that such access is provided to particularly vulnerable student groups, including migrant students, English learners, and homeless children and youths. In terms of English learners, ESSA follows the similar provisions established by Title III within ESEA and NCLB, which help ensure that SEAs and LEAs provide the appropriate and adequate programing for these students to attain English proficiency and that school personnel are trained to meet the needs of this subpopulation.

MEP Policy Goals

According to the Department of Education (DOE), the purpose of MEP is to "support high quality education programs for migratory children and help ensure that migratory children who move among the states are not penalized in any manner by disparities among states in curriculum, graduation requirements, or state academic content and student academic achievement standards" (U.S. Department of Education, n.d.). Currently, the Office of Migrant Education (OME) distributes basic funds to states using a formula that accounts for the number of migrant students in the state, ages 3–21, and each state's per pupil expenditure. These funds offer services in seven service areas with specific goals for each service area: School Readiness, English Language Arts, Math, Parental Involvement, Health Education, High School Completion, and Out-of-School Youth. As others will underscore in later chapters, the program and services are intended to supplement educational activities, and not supplant instruction or other school activities expected in the normal course of the instructional day. Thus, most activities, programs, and interventions often take place after school, on weekends, or during the summer.

The supplemental role of Migrant Education Program activities has the potential to support migrant students' educational trajectory if the program services strategically support areas of weakness in students' achievement or the school's instructional program. In order to adequately align Migrant Education Program activities with a school's curricular content, there needs to be sufficient collaboration with school districts and strategic alignment of activities and services with a school's curriculum and instruction. Precisely because Migrant Education programs are supplemental, there is also the risk that schools and/or school districts overlook their potentially important roles in supporting students' academic performance and miss collaborations with MEPs.

School Readiness

One could argue that the most significant goal of the MEP is school readiness vis-à-vis early childhood programs. Certainly, research demonstrates that access to quality preschool programs can have a lasting impact on a child's learning and socio-emotional development for kindergarten and beyond (Yoshikawa et al., 2013). Scholars have argued that access to a quality preschool program for low-income children can have a long-term impact on various outcomes, including an increase in high school completion, years of schooling, and earnings. Generally, MEP performance goals related to school readiness, including enrolling students in quality early childhood education programs and making sure kindergarten-age migrant children are ready on-time (by age 5) and enrolled in kindergarten by 5.9 years old (or less), are in sync with national policy discussions on providing universal

4   *Maria Estela Zarate et al.*

Pre-K for all children in the U.S. According to the latest California Department of Education (CDE) MEP comprehensive needs assessment, the state where the majority of migrant youth reside, almost a quarter (23%) of migrant children enrolled in kindergarten after 5.9 years of age (CDE, 2007). To complicate this issue, unfortunately, data show that the larger, Latino demographic, wherein migrant children are a small subgroup, continue to be among the least likely to be enrolled and partake in a quality Pre-K program relative to any other race/ethnicity group. To be clear, participation rates for Latino, African American, and white children are 40, 50, and 53%, respectively. These rates are further compounded by class status, where low-income students are less likely to be enrolled in preschool programs relative to their more affluent peers (U.S. Department of Education, 2015). Lack of access to an early childhood education program for migrant children has been attributed to lack of information on programs and school policies, and lack of outreach to migrant families (CDE, 2007).

English Language Arts and Math

Given most farmworker children are of Mexican descent, Spanish is the most common primary language of migrant students (Rodríguez-Valls and Kofford, this volume). Despite decades of federal policy geared toward improving literacy, bilingual education, and language development specifically for migrant families (i.e., ESEA, 1965, Improving America's School Act of 1994, Literacy Involves Families Together [LIFT] from 2000, etc.), migrant children continue to struggle with English language acquisition and development. Unfortunately, migrant farmworker students continue to lag behind their peers in English language proficiency (Ward & Fránquiz, 2004). According to the U.S. DOE, in the 2012–2013 academic year, of the 214,428 students eligible *and* participating in MEP services, 137,417 were labeled Limited English Proficient. Without doubt, English Language Learners (ELL) have lower educational attainment rates relative to their English-speaking counterparts (Gándara & Contreras, 2010).

Math proficiency rates are somewhat better than English proficiency rates for migrant youth participating in or at one point in time having participated in the MEP program. For example, when reviewing California Standards Test (CST) STAR results, an exam that was required for all public school students but is now defunct as of 2013, migrant students achieved a rating of proficient or advanced 49% of the time on the CST Math. However, on the CST English-Language Arts, migrant students in California achieved a rating of proficient or advanced only 31% of the time (California Department of Education, 2016).

Health Education and Parental Involvement

Different from other DOE supplemental programs, however, MEP also addresses broader ecological barriers beyond academic achievement. More recently, MEP programming has focused on providing health-centered programs for children and their families. According to research centered on the Migrant Health Program, "poverty status, lack of health insurance, and cultural and language barriers prevent a very large share of these workers from obtaining the health care services they need" (Villarejo, 2003). More so, many of the migrant farmworkers go without care until health problems become too acute to ignore. In recent years, MEP has taken on the same programing as the Migrant Health Program and designed preventative health services for migrant students and their families, including, but not limited to, dental health clinics, nursing intern programs, and programs to address socio-emotional issues.

Another ecological intervention addresses migrant parents' roles in supporting the education of their children. This service area is formally prescribed whereby states are required to have a parent action committee (PAC) whose role is to provide feedback and advise the program on activities and programs. In states where MEPs are organized by school district or regions, each school district or region also has its own PAC with representatives to the statewide parent committee. Although there is no comparative research on how various states and regions utilize, empower, or form PACs, we speculate that there is great variability of the roles of PACs and programs targeting parents.

High School Completion

According to Gonzalez (2013), in the first half of the 20th century, the migrant family was the cornerstone of the U.S. agricultural production system. In fact, school districts worked in tandem with agricultural companies to approve truncated elementary and secondary school schedules for migrant students so that they could help their parents (and growers) keep up with labor demand. As a result of lost instructional hours and migrant families' high mobility, educational attainment rates for children of migrant farmworkers were negatively impacted. Gonzalez (2013) asserts:

> Once the Mexican family formed into the basic unit of migratory agricultural labor, a host of consequent social conditions inevitably arose. These conditions condemned generations of Mexican children to poor nutrition, poor health, poor housing, and virtually no education. The educational pattern of migrant education was characterized by exclusion, segregation, irregular (and seasonal) attendance, and very early dropout rates.
>
> (p. 126)

The repercussions and challenges associated with the migrant lifestyle continue to be felt today. Unfortunately, current legislation allows for children aged 12 and older to work in the agricultural industry so long as work is not conducted during school hours. Per the Association of Farmworker

6 *Maria Estela Zarate et al.*

Opportunity Programs (AFOP) (2010), there are approximately 500,000 migrant students who work in fields across the U.S. The U.S. Department of Labor (2006) estimates that of all child farmworkers, 24% are between the ages of six and 13. Consequently, as one would expect, migrant farmworker students continue to have some of the highest school dropout rates in the U.S. (AFOP, 2011). While the U.S. Department of Labor estimates dropout rates as low as 37%, other scholars *optimistically* argue high school dropout rates for migrant students have hovered around 50% (AFOP, 2010; Gibson & Hidalgo, 2009). More recently, these dismal educational attainment rates can be attributed to high mobility, poverty, and health issues (Gonzalez, 2013; Nava, 2012).

Out-of-School Youth

Another example of how MEP attempts to support the unique concerns of migrant students is the Out-of-School Youth program. In this approach, the MEP appears to recognize or acquiesce to the fact that older children (typically ages 16 through 21) and young adults arrive to the U.S. with the sole intention of working as farmworkers, and with no intention of pursuing or completing formal education. Many have never attended school in the U.S. and often have very low levels of schooling achievement (Hill & Hayes, 2007). The MEP then seeks to accommodate the economic priorities of these individuals and provides counseling and resources to advance their education outside the mainstream schooling experience. For some programs, this includes English classes or vocational training. While this support is much needed in light of the economic hardships that farmworker families face that compel youth to work instead of going to school, it also reflects a national disposition and approach to migrant children that overlooks the otherwise compulsory education imperative imposed on other youth.

Transnational and U.S. Economic Contexts and Contributions

MEP is a direct appendage to broader sociopolitical issues like immigration. Although not all migrant farmworkers are immigrants, a large portion of them are, and these specific immigration trends are important and historically connected to the influx of the migrant population in the U.S. and critical to the design of policies aimed at providing services for them.

Immigration trends in the U.S. have changed during the last five decades, since the inception of ESEA. There are, however, historic trends and policies to take into account, as the majority of migrant populations are of Latina/o descent. Approximately 89% of the migrant population is Latina/o, with the majority of them migrating to California, Texas, and Florida (Coronado, 2012).

More so, the equity agenda driving ESEA centered on migrant populations is part of the Great Society programs (see Cranston-Gingras and Rivera-Singletary, this volume) and in part, a legacy of bilateral policies between the U.S. and Mexico aimed at establishing guest worker programs. For example, the *Bracero* Program established the policy levers permitting Mexican migrants to work within the U.S. (Cohen, 2011). ESEA in turn provided the levers to provide educational services for their children. The history of immigration between the U.S. and Mexico spans beyond guest worker programs in the 1940s, 50s, and 60s, but there are some key events during the last four decades that have amplified the levels of immigration of Mexican migrant farmworkers. The 1980s, after the devaluation of the Mexican peso, led to an influx of immigrants specifically from the southern state of Oaxaca. This wave of immigrants speaks an array of non-Spanish languages, including Mixtec and Zapotec, which in turn increases the complexity of learning issues for migrant populations. Not only were these new immigrants limited in the English proficiency necessary to achieve in U.S. schools, but they were also limited in Spanish, which prevented effective implementation of MEP programming, predominantly aimed at Spanish speakers (Poole, 2004). In the 1990s, the North American Free Trade Agreement (NAFTA) led to a new wave of immigration, having the same impact as the devaluation crisis of the previous decade. Moreover, NAFTA led to the increase of immigration of Mexican farmworkers as the Mexican agricultural sector struggled to compete with their subsidized American counterparts (Sears, 2014).

More recently, violence in specific parts of Central America and Mexico has also led to a new wave of immigration, specifically increasing the number of migrant children coming to the U.S. Based on data from the Migrant Policy Institute (MPI), from 1980 to 2013, the number of Central American immigrants grew from 354,000 to 3.2 million. Immigrants from El Salvador, Guatemala, and Honduras accounted for 90% of this growth. And since 2011, a growing number of unaccompanied children have arrived to the U.S. Based on data from U.S. Customs and Border Protection, during the 2014–15 fiscal year, 72,968 unaccompanied minors were apprehended on the U.S.-Mexico border (MPI, 2015).

Economic Trends and Contributions in the U.S.

The flow of immigrants from Mexico and Central and South America is an integral part of the economic fabric of the U.S. Devadoss and Luckstead (2008) assert that without a hired agricultural labor force, 80% of which is from Mexico and 96% of which is undocumented, the U.S. would not be able to carry out "critical farm tasks" (p. 879). The importance of the agricultural and farmworker labor force to the U.S. economy cannot be understated. The U.S. Department of Agriculture (2015) reports that in 2014 U.S.

8 Maria Estela Zarate et al.

farms contributed $177.2 billion to the U.S. gross domestic product. This sum is exclusive of the contributions associated with other agricultural sectors, including fishing, food, beverages, and tobacco. In another example, a report by the Udall Center for Studies in Public Policy notes that while 14% of the workforce in Arizona are immigrants, 69% are employed in the agricultural industry. It is estimated that a reduction in just 15% of this immigrant, agricultural labor force (in Arizona) would result in a loss of $600 million to the state. Across the U.S., immigrant workers generally, and farmworkers specifically, contribute millions of dollars to states' economic output and fiscal health (Gans, 2008). To be certain, the U.S. agricultural industry has demonstrated consistent output and economic growth largely as a result of improved and increased productivity levels at the hands of farmworkers (U.S. Department of Agriculture, 2015).

Interestingly, California employs about 36% of the national agricultural labor force; the largest proportion in the U.S. Over one million farmworkers are employed in seasonal labor, where roughly 40% work year-round (Martin, 2007). In other words, in California, 60% of the seasonal agricultural labor force is relegated to part-time, temporary work. As a result, farmworkers are forced to migrate to other locales to search for employment. This forced mobility has negative consequences for the education and schooling of children of migrant farmworkers and those employed in the agricultural sector.

Challenges and Barriers

Qualifying Moves

One of the most difficult and highly impactful consequences for farmworkers' families is the frequent residential mobility resulting in interrupted schooling, social alienation, and financial instability (Gonzales, 2013). When families uproot for seasonal harvests, children often have to change schools, parents have to find new housing, and new friendships are sought. Even moves within the same school district could have similar implications. Unfortunately, federal policy places stringent criteria for what constitutes a qualifying move that will allow the children to participate in the Migrant Education Program. Only moves that involved changes between school districts, administrative areas, or, depending on the geographic distance of the school district, involve a distance of 20 miles or more qualify as moves for consideration as a migrant student. Interestingly, the precise definition of a qualifying move has changed over time so that it used to be that migrant students could qualify even if they did not move within a five-year period.

The expectation of more frequent mobility can influence the impact of services on students' educational trajectories. In essence, Migrant Education Program services now have a shorter time span to effectively impact students' academic trajectory if the student and their families remain in one location longer than three years. In addition, this requirement contradicts the intuitive and mainstream goals of family stability, i.e., less mobility is better for schooling. The mobility requirement penalizes families who seek residential stability by withholding services to migrant families who prioritize residential stability whereby parents alternate picking seasons while the second parent stays home. We argue that even though a family may not be moving consistently, students whose parents are farmworkers and leave home for extended periods of time should have access to Migrant Education Program benefits even if they remain in the same school district for more than three years.

Regional staff identify potential migrant students via schools or referrals from current participants. In the identification and recruitment phase (I and R), eligibility is determined, individual learning plans are developed, and priority-for-service students are identified. Given the definition of "qualifying move," it is critical for LEAs to identify students immediately after their move. It should then not be surprising that many LEAs spend considerable resources in this phase of the migrant service program.

ELA and Math

A recent and major policy change that has implications for migrant students is the implementation of the Common Core State Standards (CCSS) in most states (National Governors Association for Best Practices, et al, 2010). These new national standards have the intention of increasing the rigor and complexity of skill and content in the areas of Math and English Language Arts (ELA). Although states are not required to adopt these standards, 33 states have implemented the standards. For migrant students, the emergence of national standards is significant given their high residential mobility rates. With the CCSS, there could be more coherence in standards and curriculum across states, lessening the impact of school changes during seasonal moves across states. It is yet unclear how consistent or aligned curriculums will be across states. Nonetheless, this aspect of the new CCSS could be a positive development for students from farmworker families.

In addition, the CCSS have sought to increase the rigor, depth, and complexity of content and skills in ELA and Math. The argument for this shift is that all students need more rigorous preparation for college work after high school. While few disagree with the goals of better preparation for college, CCSS also shifts expectations for how students will demonstrate more complex understanding of concepts, critical thinking and logical reasoning, and comprehension of more complex texts. Assessments and instructions will rely on more complex language use, and this could pose barriers for English learners without adequate scaffolding and support. Because many children of farmworker families are English learners, there could be greater challenges for them in the implementation of CCSS.

10 Maria Estela Zarate et al.

Postsecondary Education

The goal of the Migrant Education Program is "to ensure that all migrant students reach challenging academic standards and graduate with a high school diploma (or complete a GED) that prepares them for responsible citizenship, further learning, and productive employment" (U.S. Department of Education, n.d.). We observe that in this program goal, college enrollment or completion is not mentioned as an educational goal. Given current trends in human capital needs of national and global economies, we would argue that college access needs to be a part of the educational goals of the MEP (Gándara & Contreras, 2010).

To be sure, the OME also competitively distributes funds through the High School Equivalency Program (HEP) and the College Access Migrant Program (CAMP)—which are targeted to the post-high school-aged migrant population. HEP finds and provides services to migrant adults seeking to complete a high school equivalency program, and CAMP serves first-time first-year college students. These competitive funds are also supplementary and target migrant populations not captured by the basic funding formula. In the case of CAMP, students are only identified when they enroll in a college for the first time. Thus, the role of Migrant Education programs and services targeting pre-college students needs to address a current gap in service goals: increase students' preparation for and access to college.

One challenge connected to increasing college enrollment and completion for migrant youth is the lack of data available. That is, relative to elementary and high school graduation rates, migrant student college enrollment and attainment rates at the postsecondary level are not well-known. This is due, in part, to the lack of an identification or tracking system once migrant students reach the postsecondary level (Salinas & Reyes, 2004). Indeed, most of the research on migrant students has focused on the PK-12 sector and less attention, with few exceptions, has been given to migrant college access and choice research (Nuñez, 2009a, 2009b). Among the literature on migrant student college-going, much of the research focuses on the assessment and/or strengths of two primary programs—the Migrant Student Leadership Institute (MSLI) and CAMP (Araujo, 2011; Escamilla & Trevino, 2014; Ramirez, 2012). For example, Nuñez (2009b) found that MSLI is instrumental in not only fostering college enrollment but increasing the chances of students applying to selective institutions. Meanwhile, Araujo (2011) concludes that CAMP is instrumental to participants' first-year college retention.

Unfortunately, barriers that continue to hinder college access and retention for migrant students include: financial issues/concerns (Morse & Hammer, 1998; Tucker, 2000); culture shock (Duron, 1995); lack of familial support (Duron, 1995); poor high school academic preparation and/or lack of access to a rigorous college preparatory curriculum (Duron, 1995; Nuñez, 2009b); lack of English proficiency (Graff, McCain, & Gomez-Vilchis, 2013); lack of access to institutional agents (Nuñez, 2009b); high mobility (Zalaquett, McHatton, & Cranston-Gingras, 2007); and cultural/social/linguistic/ physical isolation (López, Scribner, & Mahitivanichcha, 2001; Nava, 2012; Zalaquett, McHatton, & Cranston-Gingras, 2007).

Conclusion

The current scarcity of research on farmworker families and students hinders the progress and improvement of Migrant Education programs. Farmworker students face unique and evolving schooling and educational challenges, and the ways in which the MEP addresses these challenges merit continued examination and dissemination. In the following chapters, MEP practitioners and researchers present various approaches and paradigms that they have found to be effective with migrant families and children. While this is not an exhaustive scan of the daily innovations that MEP staff and instructors generate across the country, the multiple perspectives presented here can provoke improvements and re-examinations of current practices and policies.

Note

1 Part C, Section 1309(2) of the No Child Left Behind Act defines a migratory child as someone who is or whose parents have moved in the last 36 months for the purpose of obtaining temporary or seasonal work in agriculture or fishing.

References

Acosta, R., Burch, P., Good, A. G. & Stewart, M. S. (2013). Devil is in the details: Examining equity mechanisms in supplemental educational services. In G. L. Sunderman (Ed.), *Charting reform, achieving equity in a diverse nation* (pp. 219–249). Charlotte, NC: Information Age Publishing.

Araujo, B. (2011). The college assistance migrant program: A valuable resource for migrant farmworker students. *Journal of Hispanic Higher Education, 10*(3), 252–265.

Arzubiaga, A. E., Noguerón, S. C. & Sullivan, A. L. (2009). The education of children in im/migrant families. *Review of Research in Education, 33*(1), 246–271.

Association of Farmworker Opportunity Programs (AFOP). (2010). America's farmworker children: Harvest of broken dreams. Retrieved on May 24, 2016 from http://afop.org/wp-content/uploads/2010/07/Children-in-the-Fields-Campaign-Fact-Sheet.pdf

Association of Farmworker Opportunity Programs (AFOP). (2011). Children in the fields campaign fact sheet. Retrieved on May 31, 2016 from http://afop.org/wp-content/uploads/2010/07/Americas-FW-Children-09–12–11.pdf

California Department of Education. (2007). *California migrant education program: Comprehensive needs assessment.* Sacramento, CA: Author.

California Department of Education. (2016). *2013 STAR test results.* Sacramento, CA: Author.

Cohen, D. (2011). *Braceros: Migrant citizens and transnational subjects in the postwar United States and Mexico.* Chapel Hill: University of North Carolina Press.

12 Maria Estela Zarate et al.

Coronado, R. E. (2012). *The impact of migrant education program services on migrant here-to-work out-of-school youth voices from the field.* (Doctoral dissertation, San Jose State University). Retrieved from http://csueastbay-dspace.calstate.edu/

Devadoss, S. & Luckstead, J. (2008). Contributions of immigrant farmworkers to California vegetable production. *Journal of Agricultural and Applied Economics, 40*(3), 879–894.

Duron, S. (1995). *Migrant farmworker students: Decisions involved in post-secondary participation and success.* Geneseo, NY: BOCES Geneseo Migrant Center.

Escamilla, A. & Trevino, N. G. (2014). An investigation of the factors contributing to successful completion of undergraduate degrees by the students enrolled in the college assistance migrant program. *Journal of Hispanic Higher Education, 13*(3), 158–176.

Gándara, P. & Contreras, F. (2010). *The Latino education crisis: The consequences of failed social policies.* Cambridge, MA: Harvard University Press.

Gans, J. (2008). *Immigrants and Arizona: Fiscal and economic impacts.* Tucson, AZ: Udall Center for Studies in Public Policy.

Gibson, M. A. & Hidalgo, N. D. (2009). Bridges to success in high school for migrant youth. *Teachers College Record, 111*(3), 683–711.

Gonzalez, G. G. (2013). *Chicano education in the era of segregation.* Denton, TX: University of North Texas Press.

Goodlad, J. I. & Keating, P. (1990). *Access to knowledge: An agenda for our Nation's schools.* New York: College Board Publications.

Graff, C. S., McCain, T. & Gomez-Vilchis, V. (2013). Latina resilience in higher education: Contributing factors including seasonal farmworker experiences. *Journal of Hispanic Higher Education, 12*(4), 334–344.

Hill, L. E. & Hayes, J. M. (2007). *Out-of-school immigrant youth.* San Francisco, CA: Public Policy Institute of California. Retrieved May 16, 2015 from http://www.ppic.org/content/pubs/report/R_407LHR.pdf

López, G. R., Scribner, J. D. & Mahitivanichcha, K. (2001). Redefining parental involvement: Lessons from high-performing migrant-impacted schools. *American Educational Research Journal, 38*(2), 253–288.

Martin, P. (2007). Immigration reform, agriculture, and rural communities. *Choices, 22*, 43–47.

McDonnell, L. & Hill, P. T. (1993). *Newcomers in American schools: Meeting the educational needs of immigrant youth.* Santa Monica, CA: RAND.

Morse, S. & Hammer, P. C. (1998). *Migrants students attending college: Facilitating their success.* Retrieved May 24, 2016 from http://files.eric.ed.gov/fulltext/ED423097.pdf

National Governors Association Center for Best Practices & Council of Chief State School Officers. (2010). *Common core state standards.* Washington, DC. Retrieved June 17 from http://www.corestandards.org

Nava, P. E. (2012). *Sin sacrificio no hay recompensa: Apoyo as im(migrant) parental engagement in farmworking families of the California central valley* (Doctoral dissertation). Retrieved from UCLA Electronic Theses and Dissertations. http://escholarship.org/uc/item/8mh1633q

Nuñez, A.-M. (2009a). Creating pathways to college for migrant students: Assessing a migrant outreach program. *Journal of Education for Students Placed at Risk, 14*(3), 226–237.

Nuñez, A.-M. (2009b). Migrant students' college access: Emerging evidence from the migrant student leadership institute. *Journal of Latinos and Education, 8*(3), 181–198.

Poole, S. (2004). The changing face of Mexican migrants in California: Oaxacan Mixtecs and Zapotecs in perspective. *Center for Latin American Studies and Trans Border Institute Border Brief.* Retrieved on July 3, 2016 from http://www.rohan.sdsu.edu/~latamweb/images/TBI_CLAS-Brief_OAX.pdf

Ramirez, A. D. (2012). The impact of the college assistance migrant program on migrant student academic achievement in the California state university system. *Journal of Hispanic Higher Education, 11*(1), 3–13.

Salinas, C. & Reyes, R. (2004). Graduation enhancement and postsecondary opportunities for migrant students: Issues and approaches. In C. Salinas and M. E. Fránquiz (Eds.), *Scholars in the field: The challenges of migrant education* (pp. 119–132). Charleston, WV: AEL.

Sears, N. (2014). NAFTA and its twenty-year effect on immigration. *Law and Business Review of the Americas, 20,* 669.

Tucker, L. (2000). *Fingers to the bone: United States failure to protect child farmworkers.* New York: Human Rights Watch.

U.S. Department of Agriculture. (2015). Indices of farm output, input, and total factor productivity for the United States, 1948–2013. Retrieved on June 2, 2016 from http://www.ers.usda.gov/data-products/agricultural-productivity-in-the-us.aspx

U.S. Department of Education. (2015). *A matter of equity: Preschool in America.* Washington, DC. Retrieved on June 15, 2016 from https://www2.ed.gov/documents/early-learning/matter-equity-preschool-america.pdf

U.S. Department of Education. (2016). *ED data express: Data about elementary and secondary schools in the U.S.* Retrieved June 2, 2016 from http://eddataexpress.ed.gov/state-tables-main.cfm/reportPage/newPubCustomResults

U.S. Department of Education. (n.d.). Migrant education—Basic formula grants. Retrieved on May 16, 2016 from http://www2.ed.gov/programs/mep/index.html

U.S. Department of Labor. (2006). National agricultural workers survey. Retrieved on June 2, 2016 from http://www.doleta.gov/agworker/report9/chapter1.cfm

Villarejo, D. (2003). The health of US hired farm workers. *Annual Review of Public Health, 24*(1), 175–193.

Ward, P. A. & Fránquiz, M. E. (2004). An integrated approach: Even start family literacy model for migrant families. In C. Salinas and M. E. Fránquiz (Eds.), *Scholars in the field: The challenges of migrant education* (pp. 93–109). Charleston, WV: AEL.

Yoshikawa, H., Weiland, C., Brooks-Gunn, J., Burchinal, M. R., Espinosa, L. M., Gormley, W. T., Ludwig, J., Magnuson, K. A., Phillips, D. & Zaslow, M. J. (2013). *Investing in our future: The evidence base on preschool education.* Ann Arbor, MI: Society for Research in Child Development. Retrieved on June 15, 2016 from http://fcd-us.org/sites/default/files/Evidence%20Base%20on%20Preschool%20Education%20FINAL.pdf

Zalaquett, C. P., McHatton, P. A. & Cranston-Gingras, A. (2007). Characteristics of Latina/o migrant farmworker students attending a large metropolitan university. *Journal of Hispanic Higher Education, 6*(2), 135–156.

Zong, J. & Batalova, J. (2015, September 2). Central Americans in the United States. *Migrant Policy Institute.* Retrieved from http://www. migrationpolicy.org

2 Educational Initiatives Supporting Students from Migrant Farmworker Backgrounds

Ann Cranston-Gingras and Georgina Rivera-Singletary

Historically, students from migrant farmworker families have faced significant educational challenges due to numerous factors, including frequent school changes, social isolation, cultural and linguistic differences, and the overall mismatch between school policies and the realities of the migrant lifestyle. Often identified as among those least likely to complete high school, many migrant students leave school as early as the middle grades (Cranston-Gingras, Morse, & Alvarez McHatton, 2004). For those students who are successful in high school, considerable obstacles with regard to the college admission process, financial assistance, and academic and social support often impede their attainment of a postsecondary degree (McHatton, Zalaquett, & Cranston-Gingras, 2006).

In response to these challenges and the significant disadvantages that have often characterized the educational experiences of students from migrant farmworker families, the federal government, as well as many public and private agencies, have established programs and services aimed at addressing the barriers faced by these students. In this chapter, we present an overview of select, major, nationwide education initiatives that have been developed to support students from migrant farmworker backgrounds and their families. In addition to describing the objectives and scope of a range of programs, we discuss unique and shared characteristics of the programs with implications for educational policy and practice. Particular considerations for special populations of migrant students, such as those with disabilities and English Language Learners, are also discussed. Additionally, in this chapter we profile select university centers and institutes focusing on education-related research, policy, and services for migrant students and their families and offer recommendations for future directions.

Federal Government Involvement in Migrant Education

Title I, Part C: The Education of Migratory Children

The Migrant Education Program (MEP) was established in 1966 through the reauthorization of the Elementary and Secondary Education Act (ESEA).

Prior to the MEP being written into the reauthorized ESEA, students from migrant backgrounds were provided supplemental services through Title I, Part A. However, due to the challenges impacting the education performance of migrant students, it was determined that Title I alone was not sufficient (Papamihiel, 2004). Although the federal government realized the poor performance of migrant students, the awareness of their dismal educational experiences was most notably highlighted in a documentary aired over the Thanksgiving holiday by broadcast journalist, Edward R. Murrow in 1960. In the documentary, Murrow brought national attention to the challenges students from migrant backgrounds faced, narrating the dismal conditions their families encountered daily as they worked and toiled under harsh weather conditions to harvest the fruits and vegetables that American families enjoyed at their dinner tables (Murrow, 1960).

Perhaps the most moving depiction of the migrant families were the interviews with the parents of the children regarding education. Similar to the desires of any other parent regarding their children's education, Murrow made a point to highlight the parents' sentiments regarding their vision for their children's education. Repeatedly, the parents pleaded for an equal education for their children that would lead to a lucrative career and better future life away from the fields (Murrow, 1960). Unfortunately, without a complete lifestyle change for the family, this goal seemed unachievable. The fragmented educational experiences of the children caused by the sporadic and irregular agriculture jobs of their parents were bound to contribute to the "plight" of the migrant families' daily lives and impeded their children's educational experiences. The airing of *Harvest of Shame* catapulted the educational needs of migrant students to the forefront of the American public and is credited with influencing changes in federal education legislation on their behalf (American Postal Worker, 2005).

Migrant students qualify and receive services from several federal programs designed to support students placed at risk for failure. The Elementary and Secondary Education Act (ESEA) was enacted in 1965 as part of President Lyndon B. Johnson's *Great Society Initiative*. Shortly after, in 1966, the ESEA was amended to include the Migrant Education Program (MEP), which was developed with a focus on meeting the specific educational needs of migrant students that the original legislation did not address. In the amended ESEA, the provision of educational services to migrant students was defined and specifically focused on providing education services that took into consideration the challenges that these students faced in part due to the migratory lifestyle (Papamihiel, 2004). Currently, the MEP continues to receive funding and is maintained as a separate program as the ESEA is reauthorized.

In 2001, the No Child Left Behind Act included the MEP under Title I, Part C, where it remains and is now known as Education of Migratory Children in the most recent reauthorization of the ESEA law now known as the Every Student Succeeds Act (ESSA) signed by President Obama in

16 *Ann Cranston-Gingras and Georgina Rivera-Singletary*

2015 (ESSA, 2015). ESSA (2015) is focused on a clear goal of fully preparing all students for success in college and careers. Fortunately, for the MEP, the goal of ESSA (i.e., college and career readiness) is an intended outcome for the current MEP. Most importantly, the MEP has retained its status as a standalone, categorical program designed exclusively for students from migrant backgrounds with the clear goal of fully preparing each of them for success in college and careers and ensuring they have the same opportunities as other students to meet education standards (U.S. Department of Education, 2016e).

Funding for the MEP has remained steady for years and is allocated through the U.S. Department of Education, Office of Migrant Education (OME). OME receives funding applications from states and makes the appropriation based on categorical counts of migrant students, summer intercession services, and the cost of education in each state (U.S. Department of Education, 2016g). States appropriate funds to local education agencies (LEA) through an annual grant application process that contains a comprehensive needs assessment, service provision, and budgeted activities that design services related to academic, health, and support services. The majority of the direct services to students and families are provided through the LEAs within the school setting. The MEP funds support "high quality education programs for migratory children and help ensure that migratory children who move among the states are not penalized in any manner by disparities among states in curriculum, graduation requirements, or state academic content and student academic achievement standards" (U.S. Department of Education, 2016g). For fiscal year 2015, the Department of Education reported that $374,751,000 was appropriated to the MEP for migrant education activities provided by states through local education agencies (LEA), specifically school districts (US Department of Education, 2016). Although funding is not optimal, the continuous allocation of funds for the MEP signals the high level of importance the federal government places on providing services to migrant students based on their unique educational needs.

As part of the services provided in the school setting, LEAs are also responsible for activities related to coordination among states and other programs and identification and recruitment of eligible students (an area that challenges MEP programs because of student transiency), which is the cornerstone of the MEP. As a whole, the MEP provides services to eligible migrant students that include academic instruction; remedial and compensatory instruction; bilingual and multicultural instruction; vocational instruction; career education services; special guidance; counseling and testing services; health services; and preschool services (U.S. Department of Education, 2016g). All MEP services are focused on mitigating the challenges and barriers resulting from migrancy faced by migrant students. Children and families are flagged for eligibility for MEP services as part of their school enrollment process. To qualify for the MEP, the student must be:

(3) a child or youth who made a qualifying move in the preceding 36 months

(A) as a migratory agricultural worker or a migratory fisher;
(B) with or to join, a parent or spouse who is a migratory agricultural worker or migratory fisher.

(5) Qualifying move—The term *"qualifying move"* means a move due to economic necessity-

(A) from one residence to another residence; and
(B) from one school district to another school district except-

(i) in the case of a State that is comprised of a single school district, wherein a *qualifying move* is from one administrative area to another within such district; or
(ii) in the case of a school district of more than 15,000 square miles, wherein a *qualifying move* is a distance of 20 miles or more to a temporary residence to engage in a fishing activity.

(ESSA, 2015, Title I, Part C, Education of
Migratory Children, Section 1309, Definitions)

If a child is found to be eligible for the MEP, a certificate of eligibility (COE) is completed with the pertinent information and then entered into a state data platform, which informs the counts for each state and supports records transfers among states. Once the COE process is completed, the child is identified as a migrant student and program services are provided, including coordination with other federal programs for a period of three years from identification. Two of these programs, the Title III, English Language Acquisition Program, and IDEA, Individuals with Disabilities Education Act, are discussed below.

Title III, English Language Acquisition Program

Migrant students are often classified as English Language Learners (ELL), students who speak a language other than English, and require services that support English language development or enhancement. Nationwide, 129,052 students from migrant backgrounds are also classified as ELL and qualify for both MEP and ELL program services (Ed Data Express, 2016). To address the English language development needs of ELL students, the federal government established the Office of English Language Acquisition (OELA), which is responsible for "national leadership to help ensure that English learners and immigrant students attain English proficiency and achieve academic success" through a variety of educational programs funded through the Title III, Part A, English Language Acquisition program (U.S. Department of Education, 2016c). OELA is also the governing agency that distributes federal funds to support English language acquisition instructional and culturally appropriate activities for students at the state and local level. This ELL program is funded through the federal government as a formula grant and is based on the number of Limited English proficient (LEP) and immigrant students within each state. Nationally, there are 4,931,996 students classified and enrolled in schools and participating in OELA funded programs (Ed Data Express, 2016). Similar to the MEP, OELA is responsible for receiving, reviewing, and approving state applications for funding. Once states receive funding from the federal level, LEAs apply to the state for those funds as a sub grantee if they have a local plan approved. The most recent funding appropriation information available for the program shows that in fiscal year 2012, Title III, Part A, was appropriated $732,144,000 (U.S. Department of Education, 2016d).

Historically, the English Language Acquisition program was known by its legislative nomenclature, the Bilingual Education Act (BEA). Through repeated reauthorizations, the BEA's name changed several times until in 2001, the BEA was reauthorized as part of the No Child Left Behind Act and became known as the Title III, Language Instruction for Limited English Proficient and Immigrant Students program. Under the most recent reauthorization of the ESEA into ESSA, the program is now known as the Title III Language Instruction for English Learners and Immigrant Students (ESSA, 2015). Eligibility for Title III is based on criteria that include an individual who was not born in the U.S. and whose native language is a language other than English or an individual who comes from a home where a language other than English is spoken. The goal of Title III is to provide ELL students with programming that helps increase the English language proficiency of English learners so that they can eventually be successful in English only classes. Similar to the MEP, students participating in this program are expected to "attain English language proficiency, develop high levels of academic attainment in English, and meet the same challenging standards as all children are expected to meet" (de Jong, 2011, p. 29). Therefore, it makes sense that federal programs collaborate to assist migrant students who are also English learners in achieving high academic standards. In NCLB (2001), Title III, English Language Acquisition and Enhancement Program, the following sections specify collaboration: sections 3253 3124, 3212B (vii), 3231.2 (b), (f), and (h), 3214 A (iii) coordination and collaboration between programs for students with limited English proficiency is mentioned as a critical component of effective educational services. However, a lack of collaboration among federal programs exists despite potential benefits and legislative mandates (Artiles & Harry, 2006; Keller-Allen, 2006; McCardle, Mele-McCarthy, & Leos, 2005; National Commission on Migrant Education, 1992; Pierce & Ahearn, 2007; Strong & Maralani, 1998).

For example, most recently, one of this chapter's authors studied interagency collaboration between migrant education, special education, and ELL programs in three separate school districts through in-depth interviews with administrators from each of these programs. Findings from the study showed a general lack of collaboration when providing federal program services to students identified under more than one federal program. Although participants in this study verbalized the benefits and importance of collaboration, they negated the benefits by presenting the challenges and rationalizations for not collaborating, which seemed to overshadow the perceived positive outcomes that could result (Rivera-Singletary, 2014).

Individuals with Disabilities Education Act (IDEA)

In addition to academic and other challenges posed by mobility and language differences, students from migrant farmworker backgrounds are at high risk for disabling conditions due to a variety of factors, including extreme poverty, dangerous living and working conditions, poor health care, prenatal and postnatal exposure to pesticides, and low levels of parental educational attainment (Cranston-Gingras & Paul, 2008). Compounding the problem, educators often have difficulty differentiating between English language learning needs and language/learning disabilities, causing frequent misidentification and delays in special education services (Harry, 2007; Sullivan, 2011; Wagner, Francis, & Morris, 2005). Nationwide, there are 24,974 migrant students who are dually identified as migrants and students with disabilities (Ed Data Express, 2016). Therefore, knowledge of the requirements of the Individuals with Disabilities Education Act (IDEA) and an understanding of the educational supports schools serving migrant students with disabilities are required to provide is important. For years, children with disabilities were provided educational services away from the school setting in institutions, special schools, or at home away from and isolated from their peers (Winzer, 1993). Through advocacy groups, litigated cases, and the civil rights movement, children with disabilities were purported the opportunity to be educated in settings similar to students without disabilities (Winzer, 1993; Yell, 2006).

In 1975, Public Law 94–142 (P.L. 94–142), the Education for All Handicapped Children Act, was established and paved the way for dramatic changes in the educational services provided to children with disabilities, including the setting where these services were rendered. P.L. 94–142 specifically established the right to a Free Appropriate Public Education (FAPE) for all children without regard to disability (Itkonen, 2007; Winzer, 1993). In 2004, the Education for All Handicapped Children Act was reauthorized and renamed the Individuals with Disabilities Education Act (IDEA). IDEA (2004) maintained the FAPE requirement and established that in order for a state to qualify to receive federal funds to implement the program services, they must provide an assurance regarding the inclusion of all children with disabilities regardless of the severity of the disability (Yell, 2006). In addition to maintaining the FAPE clause, the 2004 reauthorized IDEA incorporated additional parts to the Act: part A (purposes and definitions), part B (state plans for FAPE), part C (infants and toddlers), and part D (implementation, research, personnel, and professional development) (Yell, 2006).

The Office of Special Education Programs (OSEP) is the federal entity responsible for supporting special education programs for children with disabilities. States apply to OSEP for funding by outlining the processes they will follow to meet the requirements of IDEA, specifically FAPE. Part of the federal application process requires that a state design a plan outlining the assurance that all children will be provided FAPE. The absence of this plan disqualifies states from applying for federal funds (Yell, 2006). The USDOE Grants to Local Educational Agencies budget tables show that for 2015, $11,497,848,000 was appropriated for special education programs and estimate $11,912,848,000 for 2016 and $11,912,848,000 for 2017 (U.S. Department of Education, 2016d). Part of these funds is used for early identification of children who may need early intervention services for a disability, including migrant students. In regulations section 300.11, in Part C of IDEA (2004), a clause that is related to migrant students' identification requires states to find "highly mobile" children, including "migrant children," as part of their program compliance for child-finding (U.S. Department of Education, 2016f). Considering this requirement, it would make sense that special education and MEP staff collaborate to facilitate identification; however, as with migrant education and ELL, collaboration between special education and migrant education professionals is often fraught with obstacles. Although understood to be important in theory, professionals find it difficult in practice to collaborate on behalf of migrant students with disabilities (Rivera-Singletary, 2014). Factors that have been cited as making collaboration challenging for migrant education and special education professionals are related to federal and state requirements, specifically compliance with IDEA and the perceived need by special education professionals to place more weight on IDEA program specific services instead of other federal program services because of potential legal repercussions (Bayne-Smith, Mizrahi, & Garcia, 2008; Johnson, Zorn, Tam, Lamontagne, & Johnson, 2003; McWayne, Broomfield, Sidoti, & Camacho, 2008; Rivera-Singletary, 2014; Zhang, Schwartz, & Lee, 2006). Failure to recognize the advantages of working closely with specially trained staff in the Migrant Education Program in reaching migrant students with disabilities and meeting their needs seems shortsighted in light of the potential benefits.

Ancillary Program Providing Support to Students Participating in MEP: National Portable Assisted Study Sequence Program (PASS)

High school completion rates for students from migrant backgrounds have historically been among the lowest for any group of students in the nation. A major contributing factor has been the difficulty a student encounters in completing semester course work prior to moving to their family's next work location. In response to this concern, the Geneseo Migrant Center in upstate New York developed the Portable Assisted Study Sequence program (PASS). The PASS Program provides secondary migrant students the opportunity to keep up with their courses and earn academic credits through self-contained, semi-independent study courses. Students participating in PASS generally take their courses while traveling in order to make up courses, meet graduation requirements, or cope with scheduling difficulties. PASS courses are designed to parallel regular academic courses and are competency-based and learner-centered and aligned to graduation requirements nationally (Geneseo Migrant Center, 2016).

The National PASS (NPC) Center, which is housed in the Geneseo Migrant Center, was established in 1997 to serve as a national clearinghouse and coordinating center for bringing PASS courses into alignment with current academic learning standards. The NPC oversees the development of academically rigorous courses that are accessible and cost-effective for MEPs. In addition, the NPC provides support, materials, and training for program implementation and has a database of state contacts to facilitate seamless services to migrant students and MEPs. According to the most recently available data, 29 states nationally provide the PASS program to approximately 10,000 participants annually as an alternative program for secondary migrant students' credit recovery and accrual. Although the NPC does not directly receive federal funding for this initiative, part of their funding comes from federal funds provided to states for the MEP. States have the option to set aside funds to provide additional funding for LEAs who submit a separate grant application specific to providing PASS program services. In addition, state MEP offices directly pay NPC PASS license fees as part of establishing a distribution site for the PASS program (Geneseo Migrant Center, 2016).

U.S. Department of Education Discretionary Programs for Youth from Migrant and Seasonal Farmworker Backgrounds

The federal government through the U.S. Department of Education, Office of Migrant Education currently administers two discretionary grant programs for individuals from migrant and seasonal farmworker backgrounds, the High School Equivalency Program (HEP) and the College Assistance Migrant Program (CAMP). HEP and CAMP are authorized under Section 418A of the Higher Education Act and are operated in collaboration with Institutions of Higher Education (IHEs), with most housed on college and university campuses. HEP and CAMP programs are awarded to institutions through a competitive grant process on a five-year funding cycle. Although the educational attainment levels of participants in HEP and CAMP differ, the underlying mission, to provide previously unavailable educational opportunities to individuals from farmworker backgrounds, is the same for both programs.

High School Equivalency Program

The High School Equivalency Program (HEP), which has existed since 1967, assists farmworkers and their dependents in obtaining the equivalent of a high school diploma and transitioning to postsecondary education, employment, or military service. Eligible participants in the HEP program must be aged 16 and above and not enrolled in school. There are currently 43 HEP programs serving approximately 6,000 students across the country. Services provided by HEP programs include academic instruction, counseling, job placement, room and board for residential students, stipends, health care, and exposure to cultural activities. Historically, the HEP program has been very successful in meeting its performance goals. However, during fiscal year 2014, the most recent year for which outcome data are available, the percentage of HEP participants receiving their high school equivalency diploma was slightly lower in comparison to previous years (USDOE, 2015). This reduction in HEP graduates is not surprising, however, because starting in 2014, all students desiring a high school equivalency diploma have been required to take new, strictly computer-based exams requiring higher levels of critical thinking and mathematics skills. Together with technical assistance from the Office of Migrant Education, programs are making adjustments to meet these demands. With regard to placement of HEP graduates, of those HEP students who were successful in receiving their high school equivalency diploma, during the most recent year for which data are available, approximately 80% entered postsecondary education programs, attained upgraded employment, or entered the military (USDOE, 2015). Perhaps most importantly, HEP programs afford out-of-school migrant youth a renewed opportunity for educational success in a supportive environment, increasing their self-esteem and academic confidence. Further, the location of many HEP programs on college campuses provides opportunities for daily interaction with college faculty and students and integration into the higher education environment, helping HEP students envision themselves as college students.

College Assistance Migrant Program

The College Assistance Migrant Program (CAMP) began in 1972 in response to public awareness regarding the lack of higher education opportunities for the children of migrant farmworkers (National Commission on Migrant Education, 1992). CAMP programs assist students from migrant or seasonal farmworker families with college enrollment and successful completion of their first year. Services provided by CAMP include recruitment, financial assistance, academic monitoring, tutoring, access to internships, and social support. The CAMP program serves approximately 2,400 students annually, with 40 CAMP programs currently funded nationally. Willison and Jang (2009) examined reports on the progress of over 7,000 CAMP students served at 64 programs nationwide during a four-year period. They concluded that "CAMP's have demonstrated the federal program's overall capacity to assist students in successfully completing their initial year of college" (p. 259). According to a 2015 U.S. Department of Education report, the percentage of CAMP participants completing the first year of college in good standing was 86.7%, with 96.2% continuing their postsecondary education (USDOE, 2015). While the CAMP program has realized its goal of increasing access to higher education and support during the first year of college for students from migrant farmworker backgrounds, successful completion of the baccalaureate degree requires institutional commitment to ongoing support for these students. Further, CAMP participants represent a subgroup of migrant students whose academic success has positioned them to take advantage of the opportunities afforded by the program. Unfortunately, persistently high dropout rates (McHatton, Alvarez, and Cranston-Gingras, 2006; Mejia & McCarthy, 2010) and achievement gaps between migrant students and their peers (Free, Križ, & Konecnik, 2014) evidence the need for continued and intense focus on academic skills and college readiness for these students.

U.S. Department of Labor Employment and Training Administration, National Farmworker Jobs Program (NFJP)

The National Farmworker Jobs Program, which is authorized under Section 167 of the Workforce Innovation and Opportunity Act (WIOA), is designed to address unemployment and underemployment among farmworkers. The program is administered through local community organizations and state agencies, such as school districts. To qualify for the program, an individual must have worked as a seasonal farmworker or have been the dependent of a farmworker during the 12-month period prior to applying for services. Additionally, male applicants must not have violated the Military Selective Service Act and all applicants must be authorized to work in the U.S. Further, to qualify for services under the Youth subpart of the program, participants must be age 14 to 21 and also meet all other program requirements (U.S. Department of Labor, 2016). There are currently 52 employment and training focused programs nationwide funded through the NFJP and administered by public, private, and nonprofit grantees. Approximately 20,000 farmworkers are served annually through the NFJP program, with 85.5% of participants entering employment (U.S. Department of Labor, 2016). Interestingly, Clary, Ladinsky, Angus, and Millar (2013) reported that the main employment barrier for NFJP participants they studied were "educational or skill deficiencies" (p. xv) and that the majority of participants reported difficulties with the English language as a barrier to employment. While employment and occupational skills training is the primary focus of NFJP programs, basic education services can also be provided. Additionally, partnerships with community agencies and federal education programs such as the HEP can provide the opportunity for participants to receive high quality, specialized educational services such as high school equivalency exam preparation and English language development while working on occupational skills and job training. Partnerships such as this can prove especially beneficial to participants in the Youth program, since the relationship of HEP programs with colleges and universities can provide needed exposure to postsecondary environments and opportunities.

U.S. Department of Health and Human Services, Migrant and Seasonal Head Start Program

Established in 1968, the Migrant and Seasonal Head Start Program (MSHS) provides comprehensive early childhood services, including education, medical and dental care, parent involvement activities, nutrition, and social services to farmworker children and their families. To be eligible for MSHS, families must earn more than 50% of their income from agricultural work, with their total income below 100% of the federal poverty level and have at least one child under the age of six (Keefe, 2015). Approximately 32,000 children are served in MSHS in 38 states across the country (Fishman & Wille, 2014). Because of the unique needs of the migrant population, MSHS programs differ from traditional Head Start programs. For example, since farm labor involves long hours, most centers operate six days a week, opening very early in the morning and staying open into the evening to accommodate parents whose work begins before sunrise and extends into night. Further, centers often operate in accordance with the growing seasons and may only be open during certain months of the year as families move in and out of the area. According to Keefe (2015), the majority of families served in MSHS programs report that Spanish is their dominant language. Therefore, MSHS programs support students and families in Spanish while also working on English language acquisition (Mathur & Parameswaran, 2012).

University Centers Focused on Migrant Education and Research

Boise State University, Center for Multicultural Educational Opportunities

The Center for Multicultural and Educational Opportunities at Boise State University is dedicated to providing support to students from historically underrepresented groups, including those from low-income backgrounds and other non-traditional college-attending circumstances. Since 1991, addressing academic achievement issues and promoting success among students from migrant farmworker families through support programs, research, advocacy, and leadership in policy development has been a major focus of the Center. The Center currently has seven independently funded programs, including long-standing HEP and CAMP programs.

Educational Initiatives 25

Cornell University Community and Regional Development Institute Farmworker Program

The Cornell University Community and Regional Development Institute is comprised of interdisciplinary faculty and professionals dedicated to community development, including education. A major focal area of the Institute is the Farmworker Program, which has the dual mission of improving living and working conditions of farmworkers and their families, as well as recognizing and promoting the full participation and contributions of farmworkers to local communities and society. The Institute has several ongoing research and outreach strands aimed at addressing long-term challenges faced by farmworkers. These include projects focused on cultural competency and provision of health services, farmworker contributions to communities, social integration, and farmworker demographics.

Michigan State University Migrant Student Services Center

The Migrant Student Services Center at Michigan State University (MSU) was established in 2000 to provide educational opportunities for migrant students. Through a variety of programs and services, migrant students have the opportunity to complete their high school education, pursue a college degree, and participate in study abroad and career internships. Through the Center, migrant students participate in a study abroad activity in Mexico that fulfills the "global citizenship" goal of the MSU college program. MSU migrant students are also able to participate in internships to build their employability skills and gain professional knowledge in the career of their choice. Further, the MSU Center partners with the Michigan Department of Education in providing an Identification and Recruitment (ID&R) Office at the university to conduct identification and recruitment activities for Michigan school districts to complete certificates of eligibility and provide support services to migrant students and their families.

State University of New York at New Paltz, Mid-Hudson Migrant Education Outreach Program

Based at the State University of New York at New Paltz, the Mid-Hudson Migrant Outreach Center was established to support the educational success of migrant students. In partnership with parents, community, and the Education Department of the College, migrant students are provided a variety of educational services through the regular school year and in the summer. During the regular school year, educational services include advocacy and coordination with schools and community agencies, outreach activities, and academic tutoring. During the summer, the program provides in-school summer programs for elementary school students, in-home tutoring services for those that cannot attend the school programs, and PASS for secondary students who are deficient

26　*Ann Cranston-Gingras and Georgina Rivera-Singletary*

in credits. Out-of-school youth are provided the opportunity for educational programs, such as obtaining a GED through referrals to HEP, or learning or enhancing English skills. The College maximizes the services provided to migrant students by establishing interagency collaboration with the Bilingual/ ESL Technical Assistance Center (BETAC), Agri-Business Child Development Centers (ABCD), and Migrant Health. In addition to serving migrant students in school, the Center provides adult education services for other family members in their homes or at the migrant camps where families reside.

State University of New York at Oneonta, ESCORT

Established in 1986 and located at the State University of New York at Oneonta, ESCORT is a national resource center dedicated to migrant education. ESCORT partners with federal, state, and local education agencies to help improve services for migrant youth. Specifically, ESCORT provides professional development and technical assistance in areas of identification and recruitment of migrant students, language and literacy development, and program evaluation services specifically for developing the comprehensive needs assessment and service delivery plan for the MEP (ESCORT, 2016). In addition to providing technical assistance, ESCORT staff have authored instructional materials such as "Help! they don't speak English," focused on supporting educators working with secondary migrant students who are also English Language Learners, as well as numerous briefs highlighting policy, regulation, or guidance changes affecting the MEP. Further, ESCORT also maintains the National Migrant Education hotline, a service that is crucial to the MEP and the families that they serve. The hotline allows families to call for support with school enrollment and to access MEP-sponsored support services as they travel between states.

University of Colorado at Boulder, BUENO Center for Multicultural Education

Housed at the University of Colorado School of Education, the BUENO Center conducts and disseminates research, provides training, and administers service projects with a concentration on promoting quality education emphasizing cultural pluralism. While not exclusively focused on migrant education, the Center has placed heavy emphasis on work in this area since 1976. It is recognized as a leader in preparing culturally competent teachers and fostering research on bilingual and multicultural education as well as providing educational opportunities at all levels for students from migrant backgrounds.

University of South Florida, Center for Migrant Education

Established in 1987, the University of South Florida Center for Migrant Education is housed in the College of Education and partners with local, state, and national agencies and organizations to address educational challenges faced by migrant students and their families. Among the Center's initiatives are research and dissemination of new knowledge focused on practices, policy, and perspectives regarding education for migrant students (University of South Florida Center for Migrant Education, 2016). Specifically, research and programs conducted through the Center have focused on strategies for assisting students from migrant and seasonal farmworker families who have dropped out of school in continuing their education, effective practices for recruiting and supporting students from migrant and seasonal farmworker families in higher education, and contributions to understandings about education for migrant students with disabilities. In addition, the Center sponsors university scholarships and provides support to assist undergraduate students from migrant backgrounds in preparing for careers as teachers, and also to assist graduate students in becoming educational leaders.

Implications

In this chapter, we discuss major national initiatives focused on improving educational outcomes for students from migrant farmworker backgrounds. Preparing and reviewing this information has afforded an opportunity for reflection on the strengths and limitations of the present system. An important observation is that national policies, enacted through federal agencies, appear to interact effectively with state and local entities in the provision of services to migrant students and their families. In most cases, federal funding flows either through the states to local entities or directly from the federal government to local grantees, with program design and services largely influenced by federal policies. For the most part, these programs appear to be successful in providing good quality services that meet the specific needs of migrant students and their families within the guidelines of the funding agencies. However, collaboration between and among federal programs and agencies at the national, state, and local levels appears limited.

Although there are policies in place to encourage coordination of services, few incentives to do so exist. Coordination guidance from federal, state, and local education agencies tied to anticipated outcomes is needed to influence collaboration. With diminished federal rulemaking and increased flexibility for states under the reauthorized ESSA (NCLB), opportunities exist for integration of collaboration-focused accountability measures with regard to migrant eligible students with disabilities and those who are English learners. This is especially appropriate in states with high numbers of migrant students.

In addition to legal requirements for migrant students to have access to special education and English learner services, there are also practical and ethical concerns. Migrant students are general education students first, entitled to access all federal programs for which they qualify. However, they are often viewed by school personnel as "belonging" to the migrant program. Since only migrant students can be served with MEP funds, providing them with additional services through other programs is sometimes viewed as "extra" rather than necessary. Unfortunately, in this regard, collaboration is perceived as an ideal rather than the norm (Rivera-Singletary, 2014). The social ecologies of migrant students revolve around their parents' work and the need to meet basic needs on a daily basis. Migrant program staff, many of whom are from migrant backgrounds themselves, are typically highly skilled in accessing support systems which can and should complement special education and English learner programs, especially with regard to essential components such as universal screening, unbiased assessment, record transfer between states, and family involvement.

Another concern that has been discussed extensively in the migrant education community, and was readily apparent in preparing this chapter, is the lack of research related to specific national programs and initiatives. While the federal government has in recent years stepped up efforts at data collection and reporting of achievement and other outcomes in accessible formats for many of its programs, researchers have not embraced the opportunity to use available data to springboard studies within and across programs. While this scarcity of research in migrant education may be due to a lack of funding, and that needs to be addressed, it is also reflective of a practitioner-dominated field and the need to support the development of individuals who are engaged in work with migrant students to conduct research in the area.

Further, in addition to utilizing existing data for research on programs, there is a need to emphasize the use of data for continuous improvement of practice. All of the programs profiled are required to collect and report performance and other data that could inform practice. However, there is little available evidence that these data are used by practitioners to inform programmatic decisions either locally or on a larger scale.

Finally, examination of the programs profiled highlighted the continuing need for specialized programming that takes into account the unique needs of the migrant student population. However, it also reemphasized that quality education for students from migrant backgrounds at all levels must be the concern of all education personnel working together in order to realize the hopes and dreams of a better life for their children as articulated by the migrant parents interviewed in the 1960s.

References

American Postal Worker. (2005). Groundbreaking, heartbreaking, 'harvest of shame'. Retrieved on March 15, 2015 from http://www.apwu.org/laborhistory/05–3_har vestofshame/05–3_harvestofshame.htm

Artiles, A. & Harry, B. (2006). Addressing culturally and linguistically diverse student overrepresentation in special education: Guidelines for parents. Retrieved from http://www.nccrest.org/Briefs/Parent_Brief.pdf

Bayne-Smith, M., Mizrahi, T. & Garcia, M. (2008). Interdisciplinary community collaboration: perspectives of community practitioners on successful strategies. *Journal of Community Practice, 16*(3), 249–269.

Clary, E., Ladinsky, J., Angus, M. H. & Millar, A. (2013). *Evaluation of the National Farmworker Jobs Program.* Washington, DC: Mathematica Policy Research.

Cranston-Gingras, A., Morse, W. & Alvarez McHatton, P. (2004). First year college experiences of students from migrant farmworker families. *Journal of the First Year Experience and Students in Transition, 16*(1), 9–25.

Cranston-Gingras, A. & Paul, J. L. (2008). Ethics and students with disabilities from migrant farmworker families. *Rural Special Education Quarterly, 27*(1), 24–30.

de Jong, E. (2011). *Foundations of Multilingualism in Education: Principles to Practice.* Philadelphia, PA: Caslon Inc.

Education Data Express. (2016). *Data about elementary and secondary schools in the U.S.* Retrieved on May 10, 2016 from http://eddataexpress.ed.gov/data-element-explorer.cfm

ESCORT: Collaborate-Innovate-Facilitate-Educate. Retrieved on May 9, 2016 from http://escort.org/program-improvement

ESSA. (2015). Retrieved on January 1, 2016 from http://www2.ed.gov/documents/essa-act-of-1965.pdf

Every Student Succeeds Act (2015). 114th Congress, Public Law 114–95, Washington, DC.

Fishman, M. & Wille, J. (2014). *Head start CARES for migrant and seasonal families: Adapting a preschool social-emotional curriculum.* OPRE Report 2014–43. Washington, DC: Office of Planning, Research and Evaluation, Administration for Children and Families, U.S. Department of Health and Human Services.

Free, J. L., Križ, K. & Konecnik, J. (2014). Harvesting hardships: Educators' views on the challenges of migrant students and their consequences on education. *Children and Youth Services Review, 47*(Part 3), 187–197. doi:10.1016/j.childyouth.2014.08.013

Geneseo Migrant Center. The Pass Program. Retrieved on May 9, 2016 from http://migrant.net/index.html.

Harry, B. (2007). The disproportionate placement of ethnic minorities in special education. In L. Florian (Ed.), *Handbook of special education* (pp. 69–84). London: Sage.

IDEA. (2004). Retrieved on April 8, 2015 from http://idea.ed.gov/explore/home Individuals with Disabilities Education Improvement Act of 2004 (2004). 108th Congress, Public Law 108–446. Washington, DC.

Itkonen, T. (2007). PL 94–142: Policy, evolution, and landscape shift. *Issues in Teacher Education, 16*(2), 7–17.

Johnson, L., Zorn, D., Tam, B., Lamontagne, M. & Johnson, S. (2003). Stakeholders' views of factors that impact successful interagency collaboration. *Exceptional Children, 69*(2), 195–209.

Keefe, A. (2015). NAWS MSHS supplement report brief 2: Language and literacy backgrounds of MSHS-eligible parents. Brief prepared for the Office of Planning, Research and Evaluation, Administration for Children and Families, U.S. Department of Health and Human Services.

Keller-Allen, C. (2006). English language learners with disabilities: Identification and other state policies and issues. In Forum in Depth Policy Analysis. Project

Forum at National Association of State Directors of Special Education (NAS-DSE), August, 2006.

Mathur, S. & Parameswaran, G. (2012). School readiness for young migrant children: The challenge and the outlook. *ISRN Education, 2012*, 1–9. doi:10.5402/2012/847502.

McCardle, P., Mele-McCarthy, J. & Leos, K. (2005). English language learners and learning disabilities: Research agenda and implications for practice. *Learning Disabilities Research and Practice, 20*(1), 68–78.

McHatton, P., Zalaquett, C. & Cranston-Gingras, A. (2006). Achieving success: Perceptions of students from migrant farmworker families. *American Secondary Education, 34*(2), 25–39.

McWayne, C., Broomfield, M., Sidoti, J. & Camacho, N. (2008). Facilitators of and challenges to interagency collaboration: An early childhood perspective. *NHSA Dialog, 11*(2), 90–109.

Mejía, O. L. & McCarthy, C. J. (2010). Acculturative stress, depression, and anxiety in migrant farmwork college students of Mexican heritage. *International Journal of Stress Management, 17*(1), 1–20. doi:10.1037/a0018119

Murrow, E. J. (1960). Harvest of shame [Youtube Video]. Retrieved from https://www.youtube.com/watch?v=yJTVF_dya7E

National Commission on Migrant Education. (1992). *Invisible children: A portrait of migrant education in the United States.* Washington, DC: United States Government Printing Office.

No Child Left Behind Act (NCLB). (2001). *Title I, Part C, Section 1309, definitions.* Retrieved from Ed. gov, on May 10, 2016 from http://www2.ed.gov/policy/elsec/leg/esea02/index.html

Pappamihiel, E. (2004). The legislation of migrancy: Migrant education in our courts and government. In C. Salinas & M. E. Franquiz (Eds.), *Scholars in the field: The Challenges of Migrant Education* (pp. 13–27). Charleston, WV: AEL.

Pierce, L. & Ahearn, E. (2007). Highly mobile children and youth with disabilities: Policies and practices in five states. In *Forum in Depth Brief Analysis.* Project Forum at National Association of State Directors of Special Education (NAS-DSE), March, 2007.

Rivera-Singletary, Georgina. (2014). *Interagency collaboration for the provision of services to migrant children with disabilities: An exploratory study.* (Graduate Theses and Dissertations). Retrieved from http://scholarcommons.usf.edu/etd/5115

The Serve Center University of North Carolina Greensboro. (2012). *Migrant education program evaluation toolkit a tool for state migrant directors. Summer 2012.* Retrieved on May 16, 2016 from center.serve.com

Strong, M. & Maralani, V. (1998). *Farmworkers and disability: Results of a national survey.* Oakland, CA: Berkley Planning Associates.

Sullivan, A. L. (2011). Disproportionality in special education identification and placement of English language learners. *Exceptional Children, 77*(3), 317–334. University of South Florida Center for Migrant Education. Retrieved on May 9, 2016 from http://www.coedu.usf.edu/main/departments/sped/CME/CME.html

U.S. Department of Education (2015). HEP-CAMP results. Retrieved on May 5, 2016 from http://www.hepcampmeetings.com/resources/meetings/2015/annual-directors-meeting

U.S. Department of Education. (2016a). About Ed/Offices. English language acquisition program. Retrieved from Ed.gov, on May 9, 2016 from http://www2.ed.gov/programs/sfgp/funding.html. U.S. Department of Education. (2016b). Retrieved from Ed.gov, on May 9, 2016 from http://www.ed.gov/essa?src=rn

U.S. Department of Education. (2016c). Retrieved from Ed.gov, on May 9, 2016 from http://www2.ed.gov/about/offices/list/oela/index.html

U.S. Department of Education. (2016d). Retrieved from Ed.gov, on May 9, 2016 from http://www2.ed.gov/about/overview/budget/statetables/17stbyprogram.pdf

U.S. Department of Education. (2016e). Retrieved from Ed.gov, on May 10, 2016 from http://www.ed.gov/essa?src=rn

U.S. Department of Education. (2016f). Retrieved from Ed.gov, on May 16, 2016 from http://idea.ed.gov/explore/view/p/%2Croot%2Cregs%2C300%2CB%2C300%252E111%2C

U.S. Department of Labor. (2016). The National Farmworker Jobs Program. Retrieved from Ed.gov, on May 8, 2016 from https://www.doleta.gov/Farmworker/html/NFJP.cfm

Wagner, R., Francis, D. & Morris, R. (2005). Identifying English language learners with learning disabilities: Key challenges and possible approaches. *Learning Disabilities Research and Practice, 20*(1), 6–15.

Willison, S. & Jang, B. S. (2009). Are federal dollars bearing fruit? An analysis of the College Assistance Migrant Program. *Journal of Hispanic Higher Education, 8*(3), 247–262.

Winzer, M. (1993). *The history of special education: From isolation to integration.* Washington, DC: Gallaudet University Press.

Yell, M. (2006). *The law and special education*, Second Edition. Upper Saddle, NJ: Pearson Education.

Zhang, C., Schwartz, B. & Lee, H. (2006). Collaborative services for infants and toddlers with disabilities: Perspectives from professionals in an urban setting. *Early Child Development and Care, 176*(3), 299–311.

3 Helping Educators Connect with Migrant Students and Families
A Culturally Proficient Approach

Reyes L. Quezada, Fernando Rodríguez-Valls, and Randall B. Lindsey

This chapter provides a summary of our book, *Teaching and Supporting Migrant Children in Our Schools: A Culturally Proficient Approach*, designed to enhance and improve educators' effectiveness with migrant students and their families.[1] In the foreword, Roger Rosenthal, Executive Director of the Migrant Legal Action Program in Washington, D.C., opens by stating that migrant students are often called "children of the road." The sons and daughters of migrant agricultural workers, these children are defined by a mobility where they suffer disrupted and interrupted education, often leaving school before the end of the school year in the spring and returning to school after the year has begun in the late summer or fall. These children often attend multiple schools each year as their parents travel to find agricultural work in the fields and orchards in the U.S. They experience a patchwork quilt of education; a quilt that sometimes has a quilt square missing here or there (Rosenthal, 2016). This chapter will, therefore, guide educators to think deeply about their roles and responsibilities in the education of children of farmworker families. Readers will view their classrooms, schools, districts, and the migrant programs they lead in a broad and inclusive manner through the lens of Cultural Proficiency.

A Change in Demography in Our Classrooms

Basic approaches to multicultural education run the risk of overlooking this increasingly diverse student population that deserves special consideration and attention—students from immigrant backgrounds whose families toil the fields in order to provide better educational opportunities for their children, many of whom are English learning students. In 2011, 83 million people aged three and older were in our nation's schools. Of these, five million children were in nursery school, four million children in kindergarten, 33 million students in grades 1st through 8th, 17 million in 9th through 12th grades, and 24 million in college (Davis and Bauman, 2013). Further, the enrollment of English learning students in U.S. schools has surged in recent years. The 2000 language census reported that English learning students comprised 9% of the total K-12 enrollment, totaling 4,584,946 individual students (USDOE, 2010). In California, the English learning student enrollment for the 2014–15 school year was approximately 1,392,263 English learners, constituting 22.3% of the total enrollment in California public schools (CDOE, 2015).

For the most part, migrant students' needs are greater than those of English learning, non-migrant, low income, and/or ethnically diverse students. There are over 500,000 migrant students in our nation's schools. In California, the number of migrant students enrolled in the 2012–13 year was 122,145 (CDOE, 2013). According to the U.S. Department of Education (U.S. DOE), Office of Elementary and Secondary Education, Title I, Part C Migrant, 34% of all migrant students in the U.S. are English Language Learners (ELLs). In addition, 74% of the migrant children participating in Title I, Part A programs are enrolled in school-wide programs and 26% are enrolled in targeted assistance programs.

Demographic shifts across our national borders are bringing increasing numbers of migrant students from diverse linguistic backgrounds into our schools. Providing academic and social services to migrant students and their families in our nation's schools is a need yet to be addressed adequately. Educators and associated personnel who are committed, dedicated, and sensitive to the needs of children of migrant farmworkers are a paramount need in our schools. Addressing the educational and support needs of children and youth from migrant families, among the most educationally underserved in our schools today, must be a top priority for school districts and teacher pre-service and in-service programs and in updating our current teaching force (Bejarano & Valverde, 2012; Green, 2003; Mathur, 2011; Quezada, Rodríguez-Valls, & Lindsey, 2016; Vocke & Pfeiffer, 2009).

Needs of Migrant Students and Their Families

As discussed in previous chapters, children of migratory workers are federally recognized as "migrant students" if they travel with a parent or guardian who is a seasonal worker or migrant worker with the intent to work in agriculture, fishing, forestry, and plant nursery industries. While a majority of these workers travel within the U.S., there are a growing number of migrants engaging in transnational migration.

The 1998 study "Farm Workers in California" finds that farmworkers have the lowest earnings of any group; have the highest poverty rate; have the second lowest home ownership; have the lowest rate of health insurance and many health problems; are overwhelmingly Latino/Mexican; have lower educational attainment rates than any other group; and, over 69% of agricultural workers have no high school diploma. The sons and daughters of agricultural migrant workers fare little better than their parents. Migrant students are by far one of the least educated groups in California and many are not fluent English speakers (BCOE, 2012).

The DOE (2006) documented school personnel who have minimal or no training or preparation in meeting the specific needs of migrant students as

34   *Reyes L. Quezada et al.*

a contributing factor to the low performance of migrant students. Lack of support for migrant students manifests in the lack of smooth transitions from school to school; a lack of effective assessment tools for migrant students; few programs that develop skills to prepare migrant students for options beyond high school; and a lack of financial resources and support for school-wide changes (U.S. Department of Education, Migrant Education Program Annual Report: Eligibility, Participation, Services and Achievement, 2006).

Serving the educational needs of our migrant students has become a conundrum for many schools. To successfully educate migrant students, our schools must develop long-term approaches to professional development and resist reliance on discrete short-term instructional strategies. Our experiences are that instructional strategies must be learned, coached, and applied in a context where teachers and those who support teachers share the belief that they can educate migrant students and that migrant students deserve high quality instruction. Nationwide, Migrant Education programs can become pilot programs in which models of cultural proficiency are implemented with personnel trained to work with migrant students and their families. With these beliefs and practices in place, educators are equipped to use education models appropriate to their school and community needs.

Migrant students are predominantly of Latino/Mexican descent and face the same educational inadequacies, if not worse, as their urban counterparts. California has the largest number of migrant students. About 60% of California's school districts enroll migrant children, of which 98% are Latino students, less than 15% score at proficient levels in language arts, and less than 28% are proficient in math (USDOE, 2010). Involving migrant students in schools and connecting them with their school community result in lower likelihood that students drop out of school and continue another generation of low academic performance. By staying in school, migrant students are much more likely to aspire to higher education and varied career paths (USDOE, 2011).

It is imperative that PK-12 educators be equipped to serve this population that continues to be ignored and marginalized due to their status in society. While no one program can alone decrease the educational gap between migrant students and other demographic groups, it is important to introduce a variety of programs that integrate the students into the school community and improve their academic skills (Gándara, 2010). Kozoll, Osborne, and García (2003) document that migrant students' academic success is facilitated when "teachers accept students as they are, with the language they speak at home and value systems they live within" (p. 579).

Cultural Proficiency and Migrant Students

Given the growing numbers of immigrant and migrant students across the U.S., it is vital that educators, school districts/boards, and social service agencies strengthen their cultural proficiency knowledge and skills to work effectively with migrant students. Effective multicultural and culturally relevant education reaffirms these basic principles:

- A belief that educators and personnel of migrant students can learn is evidence of schools moving beyond negative stereotypes.
- Recognize that the particular teaching and learning challenges faced by migrant students and their families is foundational for use of linguistically and culturally diverse education strategies and services.
- Incorporate the language and cultural experiences of migrant students and their families into the curriculum to create culturally proficient classrooms, schools, and/or school districts.

These principles are grounded in valuing the agricultural lifestyle of migrant families and embracing native languages and cultures as assets, and are an important foundation for working with migrant students (Quezada, Lindsey, & Lindsey, 2012).

The Cultural Proficiency Conceptual Framework: Combating "Anonymization"

Our experiences indicate that policies and practices do not intentionally target migrant students for discriminatory treatment but, rather, seemingly innocuous policies and practices too often render invisible the assets students from migrant families bring to school. Migrant students become marginalized due to prevailing policies and practices devised to serve the needs of other, often mainstream, groups of students (Rodríguez-Valls & Torres, 2014). As an example, the first weeks after migrant students and their families arrive to a new school district, they often experience a sense of anonymization. Migrant students encounter new classmates, teachers, and administrators, and their parents attempt to navigate a new educational network. Sometimes, migrant students are labeled as immigrant and/or English learning students. These misconceptions and the lack of awareness of the unique nature of migratory families prevents them from receiving the required supplemental services (i.e., after-school programs, medical referrals, and tutorials) that will help them overcome the aforesaid anonymization, but most importantly to develop a sense of belonging within their new community (Rodríguez-Valls & Torres, 2014).

In stark contrast, culturally proficient educators are mindfully guided by a deeply held belief that their students deserve high quality education and that they and their colleagues have the capacity to learn how to educate their students—all of their students, with particular focus on migrant students. Examples of high quality programs operated by culturally proficient educators are: Family Biliteracy Project (FBP) and the Migrant Summer Academies (Rodríguez-Valls, Kofford, & Morales, 2012). The programs

36 *Reyes L. Quezada et al.*

are designed to enrich migrant students' learning processes with a non-traditional, student-centered curriculum that esteems communication between teachers and students. FBP promotes the idea of the whole family working together to enhance, enrich, and increase the funds of knowledge and literacies migrant families carry when moving from city to city. Both initiatives, FBP and MSA, were built following hooks' (2008) concept of engaged pedagogy, which "establishes a mutual relationship between teacher and [migrant] students that nurtures the growth of both parties, creating an atmosphere of trust and commitment" (p. 22).

The Tools of Cultural Proficiency

Constructive engagement in one's own learning in ways that benefit both educator and student can begin with mindful engagement of a set of tools designed to hone educators' core values related to educating all students and, thereby, shape their behaviors in working with students from migratory families. The Tools of Cultural Proficiency enable educators to respond effectively in cross-cultural environments by using a powerful set of four interrelated tools to guide personal and organizational change (Lindsey, Nuri Robins, & Terrell, 2009). The Tools of Cultural Proficiency are presented in Figure 3.1, The Conceptual Framework of Cultural Proficiency.

The Tool, Recognizing and Acknowledging Barriers to Cultural Proficiency, includes *systems of oppression*, *the presumption of entitlement and privilege*, an *unawareness of the need to adapt*, and *resistance to change*.

The Guiding Principles of Cultural Proficiency combat the above barriers, as they support the notion that culture is a predominant force; you cannot not have culture; people are served in varying degrees by the dominant culture; the group identity of individuals is as important as their individual identities; diversity within cultures is vast and significant; each group has unique cultural needs; the family, as defined by each culture, is the primary system of support in the education of children; marginalized populations have to be at least bicultural; inherent in cross-cultural interactions are dynamics that must be acknowledged, adjusted to, and accepted; and the school system must incorporate cultural knowledge into practice and policy making.

The Cultural Proficiency Continuum

The Cultural Proficiency Continuum provides educators a range of terms to use for identifying and overcoming the barriers of non-productive policies, practices, and individual behaviors, and replacing the barriers with core values that address socially just educational practices for educators and their schools. Culturally proficient educators mindfully and intentionally engage

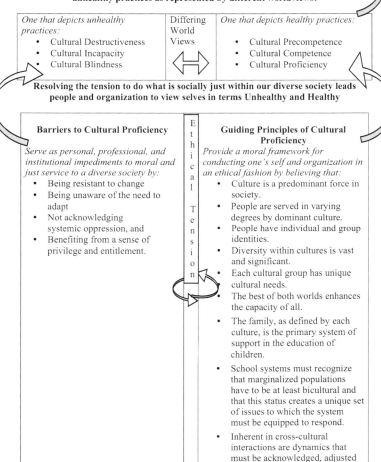

Figure 3.1 The Conceptual Framework of Cultural Proficiency

38   *Reyes L. Quezada et al.*

in their own professional learning for developing communication skills that enable them to better offer access and equitable learning opportunities for students from migrant families. The six points of the continuum describe a range of unhealthy to healthy practices for educators that serve as benchmarks to locate current practices in serving students from migratory families and to inform future possibilities as choices that result in full access and academic success in our schools. There are six points of values, behaviors, policies, and practices along the continuum. They include Cultural Destructiveness, Cultural Incapacity, and Cultural Blindness; these first three points in the continuum would be unhealthy policies and practices that exist within educational systems as well as in individuals' values, behaviors, and beliefs. The next three points in the continuum are informed by the Guiding Principles and progress from Cultural Precompetence, to Cultural Competence, and to Cultural Proficiency. These points in the continuum would be healthy policies and practices that exist within educational systems as well as in individuals' values, behaviors, and beliefs.

The Essential Elements, which are described in more detail in the following sections, serve as behavioral standards for educators, enabling them to become culturally competent in their work with migrant students as well as in the policies and practices that schools implement—they include: Assessing Cultural Knowledge; Valuing Diversity; Managing the Dynamics of Difference; Adapting to Diversity; and Institutionalizing Cultural Knowledge (Cross et al., 1989; Lindsey, Nuri Robins, & Terrell, 2009).

Assessing Cultural Knowledge

Transformative educators working with migrant students and their families acknowledge and assess their own language and cultural knowledge and the transformative processes in schools, and they learn about the many communities served by schools and/or districts. What we know about our own cultural and language heritage is an indication of our willingness to learn about migrant students and their families, their communities, as well as learning about the cultural and language heritage of our colleagues.

Educators ask: How and what steps can we take to learn about migrant farmworker families, their children, and the cultural and language assets they will bring to the school and the community? How can we assess our language and cultural knowledge about the linguistic and cultural assets of those from indigenous backgrounds? How would we start to learn what we know or do not know about the migrant farmworker families and the assets the children bring to our school? How can we lead our own and our colleagues' learning? These questions are important in guiding our own self-reflection and promoting dialogue among members of the school and the community at large. Our role as educators is to create an educational system that promotes equitable and socially just teaching practices in our classrooms and across our schools, school districts, and our community.

Sonia Nieto, along with her colleague Patty Bode (2006), defines social justice as "both a philosophy and actions that embody treating all people with fairness, respect, dignity, and generosity" (p. 2). Our role as educators is to facilitate our and our schools' professional learning and serve as educators who lead, not follow. Therefore, assessing one's cultural knowledge is essential in the inside-out journey of recognizing our role as culturally proficient educators to make our classrooms, schools, and community a safe learning place for our migrant families and their children.

Due to their mobile nature, there are effective educator practices to be considered when working with migrant students and their families. Socially just practices fully engage families and, in particular for Priority for Services (PFS) children. MEP funds must first address the needs of PFS migrant children who are failing, or at risk of failing, so they can meet the state's academic content and achievement standards, and whose education has been interrupted during the regular school year or in their educational experiences. Schools serving migrant families need:

- educators knowledgeable, in authentic ways, of the migrant lifestyle and how students being migratory might impede educators' own learning about migrant students' culture and students' prior experiences;
- educators who advocate for migrant families and embrace their migratory community as a familial capital asset through valuing the heritage and history of migrant children's family. It is important to know and utilize local, state, and national programs, as well as all school resources available to migrant families, in order to provide opportunities for success;
- educators who know how other educators, the school community, and the community as a whole react to migrant families, their children, and communities;
- educators who continuously learn how to be effective in serving their multiple migrant farmworkers' diverse communities—both domestic and families from other countries who serve as migrant seasonal workers. These may include many linguistic and culturally diverse indigenous communities;
- educators who lead their school and its grade levels and departments by modeling and promoting culturally relevant and responsive methods of instruction to meet the learning needs of migrant students; and
- educators who have the highest of expectations and utilize cooperative groups in their classrooms and support their students through ascending learning transitions by providing safe learning spaces for migrant students (Banks & Parks, 2010; Gay, 2000; Ladson-Billings, 1995; Mathur, 2011; Nieto, 2006, 2013).

These practices and roles represent paradigmatic shifts in educators' transformative learning based in acquiring deep knowledge of community needs

40 Reyes L. Quezada et al.

derived through personal, face-to-face interactions with members of migrant communities. Being knowledgeable about and valuing new or growing migratory communities being served by schools, in contrast to the cultural composition the school used to have or that they wish they had, makes educators fully capable of rethinking their practices in ways that move:

- *from* remedial programs that promote language and cultural assimilation of migrant students into the dominant culture in ways that disavow any positive influence of students' home languages and cultures
- *to* using students' migrant culture and native language as assets from which to build and promote academic and social success.

Valuing Diversity

Becoming knowledgeable about the cultural and linguistic student populations in our school and community provides the basis for valuing the assets that cultural and linguistic diversity contribute to the school and the community. The challenge for educators is committing to learning about the varied experiences of immigrant migratory families that often represent many indigenous cultures and languages.

Being engaged in professional learning about migrant populations is the first of two steps in addressing educational access and achievement disparities. Professional learning focused on migrant community culture serves to demystify groups with whom we may have had limited contact in the past. Equipped with knowledge about migrant communities, we are then prepared to align our and our schools' beliefs with high academic expectations, as well as maintaining rigorous standards of positive outcomes for the PFS migrant student population in our PK-12 schools. Inclusive belief systems regarding migrant students also extend to the out-of-school youth and migrant farmworker families in our schools. Anderson (2014) notes with respect to inclusive schools, "equity and diversity need to be embedded into the many facets of education: staff, pedagogical practices, communication, leadership, assessment, curriculum, and community engagement" (p. 12).

A culturally competent/proficient educator requires the promotion of equitable access and inclusion type programs. Such programs provide strategies, resources, and policies that provide an unobstructed entrance into, involvement of, and full participation for linguistically and culturally diverse migrant students and their families in schools, programs, and activities to reduce and eliminate academic access and achievement gaps. Educators and schools should promote equitable and socially just treatment of migrant students and partnerships with their families in an environment of acceptance, respect, support, safety, and security, such that migrant students feel challenged to become invested in the pursuits of learning and excellence without fear of threat, humiliation, danger, or disregard for who they are as migrant students.

In expressly valuing the diversity that migrant students and their families bring to school, educators can fully engage families in their children's education. Families representing language, cultural, and migratory realities different from the school too often participate at a minimal level in school activities. To preclude ignoring migratory students in the educational process, professional learning communities can be a vehicle that brings together teachers, principals, and staff along with students, parents, and community partners to emphasize teamwork and school improvement to increase student-learning opportunities (Epstein & Salinas, 2004). Epstein (2011) provides a framework of four new directions for organizing and conducting effective school, family, and community partnerships to fully engage families that contribute to student success in schools. The four directions can assist educators to forthrightly value the cultural assets that migrant students and their families bring to schools. They include:

Teamwork for Program Development—Effective program development requires a full team approach of educators, teachers, counselors, administrators, and other school personnel. Families and community partners develop comprehensive programs to meet the needs of migrant families and their children to fully engage students in goal-linked activities.

Migrant families that might not be at a school for an entire academic school year should not be precluded from leadership roles where their voices are represented in planning activities. These activities can integrate both at-home and at-school activities. The activities might involve migrant farmworker parents in the construction and care of a school-community garden or parents from the various indigenous cultural groups whose native and colorful clothing requires a particular stitch or sewing skills, or traditional cooking from their native regional and geographical areas. These can be inclusive activities for raising school funds where migrant students attend where limited educational resources are available. District, Region, and State Parent Advisory Councils provide leadership opportunities for presenting, modeling, and promoting culturally responsive techniques to meet the educational needs of linguistically and culturally diverse migrant student communities.

Goal-linked Partnerships—It is important to engage families in planned activities that connect and contribute to improving the academic achievement of migrant students and that provide safe learning spaces that foster students developing positive attitudes towards school. If migrant students are not proficient in literacy, math, or science skills, it is important for educators and schools to plan family-friendly activities that may support them at home and that provide user-friendly activities where families may support their children, even when parents and other family members may not speak English. Jeynes' (2012) research study informs us that when schools and districts are engaged in goal-linked partnership practices, student learning and motivation is enhanced, there is an increase in attendance, and

42 *Reyes L. Quezada et al.*

student misbehavior is reduced. Goal-linked activities can be accomplished by engaging educators, the school, the district, and migrant families through migrant Parent Advisory Councils and community-based resources in a collaborative manner that engages them as partners in the education of all students. Such structures often lead to strong migrant Regional Applications and/or District Service Agreements (USDOE, 2011).

Equitable Partnerships—Equity among parents, school, district, and community groups entails planning activities to reach all families—even those deemed to be "hard to reach" families. Educators must demonstrate a will for engaging in partnerships. Educators need to devise mechanisms to provide implementation benchmarks and to assess the progress of family engagement programs. Educators can no longer afford to plan family engagement programs as a "single shot" activity to accommodate one group of parents. Activities such as the four new directions lend special importance for educators to assess their own cultural knowledge. Genuine knowledge about our diverse communities provides opportunity to authentically express value for the diversity within our schools.

Culturally proficient educators strive to support migrant farmworker families in meeting their needs and the right to be equitable partners with the communities and schools where their children attend. Epstein's four directions are to support educators in developing and maintaining school-family and community partnerships as a way of communicating with migrant families and, perhaps more importantly, will serve also as an equitable and culturally proficient manner for reaching all families.

Managing the Dynamics of Difference

Migrant students and their families epitomize a vast array of cultures and languages. They speak a variety of indigenous languages—Mixteco, Zapoteco, Trique—and within these languages a scope of linguistic variances, such as Mixteco from Tezoatlán, Mixteco from Yosondúa, or Mixteco from Xochapa peacefully coexist and identify each group as culturally and linguistically unique. Educators working with and learning from migrant communities must be aware and cognizant of this uniqueness and how the funds of linguistic and cultural knowledge can enrich and contextualize the programs and services provided to students and their families (Gay, 2000). Appreciation and respect for migrant families comes from an inner dialogue in which educators reflect on their own biases and misconceptions. As Delpit (2005) points out, "We educators set out to teach, but how can we reach the worlds of others when we don't even know they exist?" (p. xxiv). The challenge is to find these worlds where migrant communities live, learn, and belong.

These worlds might exist and coexist within the communities where educators live; however, oftentimes, the migrant world remains anonymous and distant from the reality educators face on a daily basis. Educators might drive back and forth through highways that cross many agricultural fields where migrant families work to obtain an income. Yet once educators arrive at the school site or the community center, teaching and learning stand isolated from the fields on both sides of those highways. It takes a conscious and humble act of willingness to enrich teaching and learning with the migrant world. Holmes (2013) summarizes the invisibleness of migrant workers in his 2014 Margaret Mead Award winning book *Fresh Fruit, Broken Bodies*, where he states:

> Early in my fieldwork, I began to notice the segregation of workers in U.S. agriculture into a hierarchy of perceived ethnicity and citizenship. I observed economic inequalities and social hierarchies producing displacement, migration, sickness, and suffering. . . . I noticed several ways in which social and health inequalities had become considered normal, natural, and justified. I became discouraged by what appeared to be a depressing situation without any possibility for change
>
> (p. 182)

Culturally proficient educators encourage and lead conversations around the memories and experiences migrant communities bring to the programs and services designed and implemented by Migrant Education Offices. Moreover, those who are attuned to appreciating the value of such memories and stories must rise as advocates to defend and validate the cultural and linguistic diversity of all migrant students and their families.

Prominent researchers have analyzed the challenges and key factors educators face in the development of successful and effective Migrant Education programs. Among the factors identified in these studies, there are three common elements that impact the functioning and sustainability of Migrant Education programs: 1) the insufficient cohesiveness across different agencies to support students and families in overcoming the lack of belonging, anonymization, and high mobility; 2) the dearth of preparation among personnel to understand the unique needs of migrants students and their families; and 3) the need for appropriate programs and assessment tools designed specifically to meet, evaluate, and support the academic and social success of migrant students and their families (Gibson & Bejinez, 2002; Gibson & Hidalgo, 2009; Rodríguez-Valls, Kofford, & Morales, 2012).

The manner in which educators and their schools successfully manage the dynamics of differences occasioned between their own reality and the migrant world leads to effective practices at the school district level. Effectively managing the dynamics of difference honors the cultural assets each educator brings to migrant programs. Whether teachers working in the same school design an after-school program focusing on study skills or teachers from different schools work together in a Summer Program with an emphasis on how Science, Technology, Engineering, Art, and Mathematics are connected to the migrant community, all educators recognize they have a common goal; namely, an inclusive program that leads to successful outcomes for all students. Epstein (2011) underlines in her work on educational partnerships that educators and staff must "recognize shared responsibilities of home, school and [migrant] community for [migrant] children's learning and development" (p. 11). Developing effective practices when working with migrant students calls for a cohesive effort from school district personnel.

A key to building coherence and consistency in Migrant Education programs begins by having a solid leadership that manages the pedagogical differences that may exist among teachers and staff. To recognize, value, and manage such differences, administrators must create spaces—via professional development and learning—in which all personnel involved in Migrant Education programs examine their individual pedagogies and approaches when working with migrant students and their families. Administrators' roles are pivotal. The strength and effectiveness of programs require what Linsky and Heifetz (2002) define as dangerous, but needed, dialogues where the "values, beliefs, or habits of a lifetime" (p. 12) of individuals are being questioned and where each person participating in these dialogues feels empowered to "tell people what they need to hear rather than what they want to hear" (p.12).

A culturally proficient educator is one who has the courage to lead conversations that model challenging their assumptions and thoughts about students. Further, the culturally proficient educator takes steps deemed necessary to provide the best practices and services to migrant students and their families. Walking these steps, the culturally proficient educator recognizes the need for linking goals, objectives, and outcomes across practices and from all educators. As Palmer (2007) points out, "good teachers possess a capacity for connectedness. They are able to weave a complex web of connection among themselves, their subjects and their students so that student can learn to weave a world for themselves" (p.11). If we were to rephrase Palmer's thoughts, we would say educators working in Migrant Education programs must be able and willing to meet the needs of all migrant students and families. In doing so, they stop the cycle of societal and educational injustices infringed upon migrant communities. They are problem-solvers willing to mediate, knowing that "although you [they] may see with clarity and passion a promising future of progress and gain, people will see with equal passion the losses you [they] are asking them to sustain" (Linsky & Heifetz, 2002, p. 12). Mediating in ways that colleagues eventually understand that what they viewed as "loss" is, in fact, expanding their repertoire of skills and knowledge that enables them to experience success with students from various cultural communities.

Adapting to Diversity

The Cultural Proficiency Continuum displays a range of negative to positive viewpoints that reveal an inside-out approach in planning for personal and organizational growth. Culturally competent approaches embrace adapting to diversity through renewing and invigorating our commitment to support migrant students and their families more effectively. Culturally proficient educators approach educational reform initiatives such as No Child Left Behind, Race to the Top, Common Core, and the new Every Student Succeeds Act of 2015 (USDOE, 2015) in ways that guarantee a focus on ethnically diverse student populations. Although there are safeguards in the Every Student Succeeds Act of 2015 to analyze access and achievement data relative to low-income students, students of color, and English Language Learners, it is educators' responsibility to address one's and colleagues' attitudes and behaviors in working with and educating linguistically and culturally diverse migrant students and families. It is an educator's duty to challenge historical deficit-based attitudes that remain deeply embedded and integrated in our educator, school, and organizational practices. Educators must adapt asset-based approaches that foster continuous learning in terms of embracing and embedding equitable and socially just instructional and institutional policies and practices.

Adapting to diversity is an essential element of cultural proficiency's inside-out approach to change that addresses the educational needs of migrant students and their families. For too long migrant students and their families have had to blindly adapt to the norms of schools and the dominant culture that most often lead to an ever widening academic achievement gap. The respected researcher Cummins (2000) refers to the old, unsuccessful approach or way of thinking as an attitude "to ensure students remain within predetermined cultural and intellectual boundaries" (p. 284).

There are many ways we as educators adapt to diversity. We commit to learning and using the languages and cultures of the migrant communities served by our schools. Learning and integrating the cultural knowledge, language abilities, customs, and practices in both curriculum and program development is a way to learn and acquire the core of the funds of knowledge, the important resources that migrant students and their families bring to our schools (Gonzalez, Moll, & Amanti, 2005). Banks and Park (2010) frame Adapting to Diversity to be a shift in a "cultural paradigm" from thinking about ethnic minority students from a negative focus to an "assets-based perspective." This transcends to an often-prevalent deficit view of migrant students and their families and other ethnic minority students. As educators we commit to professionally, personally, and organizationally taking time to learn what is needed to ensure the academic and personal and social success for our linguistically and culturally and diverse migrant student populations. Why? Because funds of knowledge as a concept supports the importance of educators needing to know about the students they

46   *Reyes L. Quezada et al.*

serve "culturally (which) is not the same as knowing them psychologically" (Penetito, 2001, p. 20).

Institutionalizing Cultural Knowledge

Within the Migrant Education Program context, institutionalizing cultural knowledge is evident in educators' conduct and in schools' socially just policies and practices that address educational inequities and tend to close access, opportunity, and achievement gaps expressed in cultural and demographic terms. Culturally proficient educators advocate for equitable, socially just policies and practices. Data are used to inform educator and school practices in service of migrant student and family needs. Using Individual Learning Plans as benchmarks, one advocates for socially just and equitable policies and practices in use of College to Career Readiness and academic data to inform educators of migrant student needs with particular emphasis on OSY and PFS migrant students who are linguistically and culturally diverse. Educators use College to Career Readiness and other academic data to benchmark school progress in narrowing and closing academic achievement gaps of their linguistically and culturally diverse populations of OSY and PFS migrant students. Culturally proficient educators coach colleagues and community members to develop and use Regional Applications, District Service Agreements, and Comprehensive Needs Assessments and Family Biliteracy and School Readiness Programs and inform them about culturally proficient communication strategies to facilitate an understanding among the larger community in meeting the needs of linguistically and culturally diverse migrant students. Culturally proficient educators integrate the Innovative Educational Technologies system to increase the academic achievement of migrant students. Culturally proficient educators provide support systems and academic opportunities so that all secondary migrant students meet the academic standards to graduate with a high school diploma, or complete a GED, that prepares them to be College and Career Ready to be admitted to an institution of higher education so they continue to be responsible and productive citizens and increase their employment opportunities. Culturally proficient educators also institutionalize an array of Migrant Education programs to support elementary, secondary, and college migrant students after funding (in some instances) has been depleted or no longer available, such as the College Assistance Migrant program, the High School Equivalency Program, or the California Migrant Mini-Corps.

Closing Thoughts in Support of the Education of Migrant Students and Their Families

In order to continue on our journey to becoming *culturally proficient* we, as authors, educators, and community members involved in supporting educational and social justice issues of equity and access for migrant students and their families, and in the education of culturally and linguistic minority students, commit to continue as partners with PK-12 educators as *professional community learners.* We invite readers to share success stories, questions, challenges as well as personal and professional triumphs experienced in instructing and working with migrant students. We believe our PK-12 colleagues have committed their careers to serving migrant students and their families so that they may experience access and success. We look forward to being engaged in continuous dialogue so we may learn together and attain the goal of a truly inclusive socially just and equitable society.

Note

1 We would like to thank our publisher, Rowman and Littlefield Group, Inc., for allowing us to integrate these excerpts from our book. *Teaching and Supporting Migrant Children in Our Schools: A Culturally Proficient Approach* is available at www.rowman.com.

References

Anderson, M. (2014). Diversity matters. *Leadership, 44*(2), 12–15.

Banks, J. A. & Park, C. (2010). Race, ethnicity, and education: The search for explanations. In P. Hill Collins & J. Solomos (Eds.), *The sage handbook of race and ethnic studies* (pp. 383–414). London: Sage.

Bejarano, C. & Valverde, M. (2012). From the fields to the university: Charting educational access and success for farmworker students using a community cultural wealth framework. *Association of Mexican American Journal, 6*(2), 22–29.

Butte County Office of Education (BCOE). (2012). *2010–2011 Annual evaluation report: California mini-corps.* Sacramento, CA: Author.

California Department of Education (CDOE). (2013). California public school enrollment-district report. Retrieved April 1, 2015, from CDE Website http://data1.cde.ca.gov/dataquest/

California Department of Education (CDOE). (2015). California public school enrollment-district report. Retrieved on May 22, 2016, from CDE Website http://www.cde.ca.gov/ds/sd/cb/cefelfacts.asp

Cross, T. L., Bazron, B. J., Dennis, K. W. & Isaacs, M. R. (1989). *Toward a culturally competent system of care.* Washington, DC: Georgetown University Child Development Program, Child and Adolescent Service System Program.

Cummins, J. (2000). *Language, power, and pedagogy: Bilingual children in the crossfire.* Clevedon, UK: Multilingual Matters.

Davis, J. & Bauman, K. (2013). School enrollment in the United States: 2011. Retrieved on May 7, 2016 from https://www.census.gov/prod/2013pubs/p20–571.pdf

Delpit, L. (2005). *Other's people children: Cultural conflict in the classroom.* New York: The New Press.

Epstein, J. L. (2011). *School, family, and community partnerships: Preparing educators and improving schools,* Second Edition. Boulder, CO: Westview Press.

Epstein, J. L. & Salinas, K. (2004). Schools as learning communities. *Educational Leadership, 61*(8), 12–18.

48 Reyes L. Quezada et al.

Gándara, C. P. (2010, February). The Latino education crisis. *Meeting Students Where They Are, 67*(5), 24–30. *Educational Leadership*. Web. 5 Dec. 2011.

Gay, G. (2000). *Culturally responsive teaching: Theory, research, and practice*. New York: Teachers College Press.

Gibson, M. A. & Bejinez, L. F. (2002). Dropout prevention: How migrant education supports Mexican youth. *The Journal of Latinos in Education, 1*(3), 155–175.

Gibson, M. A. & Hidalgo, N. (2009). Bridges to success in high school for migrant youth. *Teachers College Record, 111*(3), 683–711.

Gonzalez, N., Moll, L. & Amanti, C. (2005). Introduction: Theorizing practices. In N. Gonzalez, L. C. Moll, & C. Amanti (Eds.), *Funds of knowledge: Theorizing practices in households, communities and classrooms* (pp. 1–28). Mahwah, NJ: Lawrence.

Green, E. P. (2003). The undocumented: Educating the children of migrant workers in America. *Bilingual Research Journal, 27*(1), 51–71.

Holmes, M. S. (2013). *Fresh fruits, broken bodies-migrant workers in the United States*. Berkeley, CA: University of California Press.

hooks, b. (2008). *Belonging: A culture of place*. New York: Routledge.

Jeynes, W. (2012). A meta-analysis of the efficacy of different types of parental involvement programs for urban students. *Urban Education, 47*, 706–742.

Kozoll, R. H., Osborne, M. D. & García, G. E. (2003). Migrant worker children: Conceptions of homelessness and implications for education. *Qualitative Studies in Education, 16*(4), 567–585.

Ladson-Billings, G. (1995). But that's just good teaching! The case for culturally relevant pedagogy. *Theory into Practice, 31*, 160–166.

Lindsey, B. R., Nuri Robins, K. & Terrell, D. R. (2009). *Cultural proficiency: A manual for school Leaders*, Third Edition. Thousand Oaks, CA: Corwin.

Linsky, M. & Heifetz, R. A. (2002). *Leadership on the line: Staying alive through the dangers of leading*. Boston, MA: Harvard Business Review Press.

Mathur, S. (2011). Educating the migrant child: Professional development for teachers of young children of seasonal farm workers. *The Journal of Multiculturalism in Education, 7*(3), 1–16.

Nieto, S. (2006). *Teaching as political work: Learning from courageous and caring teachers*. Bronxville, NY: Child Development Institute. Sarah Lawrence College. The Longfellow Lecture Occasional Papers.

Nieto, S. (2013). *Finding joy in teaching students of diverse backgrounds: Culturally responsive and socially just practices in U.S. classrooms*. Portsmouth, NH: Heinemann.

Palmer, P. J. (2007). *The courage to teach: Exploring the inner landscape of a teachers life*, 10th Anniversary Edition. San Francisco: Jossey-Bass.

Penetito, W. (2001). If only we knew. . . contextualizing Māori knowledge. In B. Webber & L. Mitchell (Eds.), *Early childhood education for a democratic society: Conference proceedings* (pp. 17–25). Wellington, New Zealand: Council for Educational Research.

Quezada, L. R., Lindsey, R. & Lindsey, D. (2012). *Culturally proficient practice Supporting educators of English learning students*. Thousand Oaks, CA: Corwin Press.

Quezada, L. R., Rodríguez-Valls, F. & Lindsey, R. (2016). *Teaching and supporting migrant children in our schools: A culturally proficient approach*. Lanham, MD: Rowman & Littlefield Publishing Group, Inc.

Rodríguez-Valls, F., Kofford, S. & Morales, E. (2012). Graffiti walls: Migrant students and the art of communicative languages. *Journal of Social Theory in Art Education, 32,* 96–111.

Rodríguez-Valls, F. & Torres, C. (2014). Partnerships and networks in migrant education: Empowering migrant families to support their children's success. *Multicultural Education, 21*(3 & 4), 34–38.

Rosenthal, R. (2016). Forward. In R. L. Quezada, F. Rodríguez-Valls, & R. Lindsey, (Eds.). *Teaching and supporting migrant children in our schools: A culturally proficient approach.* Lanham: MD: Rowman & Littlefield Publishing Group, Inc.

U.S. Department of Education. (2006). Migrant Education Program Annual Report: Eligibility, Participation, Services and Achievement. Washington, DC.

U.S. Department of Education. (2011). *Office of the under secretary, planning and evaluation service, elementary and secondary education division, The Same High Standards for Migrant Students: Holding Title I Schools Accountable*, Executive Summary, Washington, DC, 2002.

U.S. Department of Education. (2015). Every student succeed act. Retrieved on December 15, 2015 from http://www.ed.gov/essa

U.S. Department of Education, National Center for Education Statistics. (2010). *The condition of education.* 2010 (NCES 2010–028), Indicator 5.

Vocke, S. K. & Pfeiffer, S. A. (2009). Building community for migrant education services through family literacy and farm worker outreach. *The Tapestry Journal, 1*(1), 30–39.

4 *Nuestra Familia es Nuestra Fuerza*
Building on the Strengths of Migrant Families Towards School Success

Pablo Jasis and Alejandro González

Efforts to provide educational services in a systematic manner for migrant students and families can be traced to the 1960s and are commonly associated with the federal government's War on Poverty programs. Given its many years of existence, there is a relative scarcity of relevant literature on migrant education efforts from that earlier context, especially considering the potential wealth of accumulated educational experience from federal and state educational programs focused on the migrant student population. More recently, there has been a renewed interest by educational researchers and practitioners in examining effective practices, and on investigating comprehensive approaches to the educational services for migrant students and families (Jasis & Marriott, 2010; Martinez & Cranston-Gingras,1996; Romanowsky, 2003).

Consistent with earlier approaches towards migrant communities, much of the literature on migrant education from the 60s, 70s, and 80s focused on identifying and remedying perceived educational needs and social deficiencies among this student population. This tendency could be aptly characterized as saving the poor from themselves and their communities, and it was related to the "culture of poverty" approach that dominated policy narratives towards oppressed communities (Moynihan, 1969). It also mirrored the state of social awareness of American society at the time, which during the peak of the Civil Rights movement suddenly "discovered" the harsh working and living conditions of agricultural workers and their families and the workers' socioeconomic and educational vulnerability. That state of consciousness was, however, significantly impacted at the national level by the historical struggles of farmworker communities for better wages and working conditions, improved schools and opportunities for health care and social mobility, and increased civic participation and self-determination. It was precisely the mobilization of the farmworker communities, particularly in the Southwest, their struggle for union organizing, and the increasing visibility of their journey towards social justice that motivated social scientists and educational researchers to focus on the socio-cultural and ideological assets of these communities, rather than on their misperceived cultural deficits (Gonzalez, 1994). In the educational arena, this progressive trend has focused on the pedagogical value of the migrant community's emerging sense of empowerment and leadership development. The Migrant Education Program (MEP), initiated by the federal government in the 1960s, played a pivotal role in the educational lives of many migrant and seasonal agricultural communities throughout the U.S. Through different junctures, and depending on the local context, MEP has been instrumental in creating a positive space for migrant students in many school districts by providing a variety of support programs, professional training opportunities for teachers, and promoting leadership among migrant students, parents, and educators.

Most programs and activities offered by MEP have been provided in the spirit and the manner of *service* (Jasis, 2013), that is, through a relational dynamic of a *provider-recipient* model. Through this service model, the *provider* develops a sense of the recipient's needs and *provides* goods or services accordingly. Though the program may end up effectively addressing the recipient's needs—in this case the migrant community—the aim and the perspectives of this study correspond to a model of *empowerment*. In the words of Cruickshank (1999), an *empowerment* stance involves the examination of a socio-historical phenomenon through a pedagogical and ethical lens that focuses on challenging "the basic power relationships in our society. Beginning when people change their ideas about the causes of their powerlessness, when they recognize the systematic forces that oppress them and act to change the conditions of their lives" (p. 70). As a result, there are critical differences between a model of *service* and a model of *empowerment*.

Consistent with an empowerment perspective, this study examines the narratives of migrant farmworkers and their families in a small number of Southern California communities, and their relationship to the schooling of their children. This chapter is an effort to contribute to the emerging body of literature that connects the educational process of historically underserved communities to a more comprehensive analysis of their struggle for social justice and educational rights (Rogers & Orr, 2011). This study will address the following questions:

a) What are the socio-historical and ideological factors impacting the relationship of migrant farmworker parents and the schooling of their children?
b) What are the visions, contexts, and historical trends that promote leadership development and increased participation among migrant farmworkers as related to their process of educational partnership with schools?

Southern California's Invisible Neighbors

Migrant farmworkers in the Southern California region are often called the *invisible neighbors*, because their contributions to society, aspirations,

52   Pablo Jasis and Alejandro González

challenges, socioeconomic contexts, and indeed their mere presence in the area are often overlooked (Chávez, 1982). In a vast geographical region with a highly diversified economy, often seen as dominated by the technology, financial, and entertainment industries, agriculture is still an economic mainstay of the state. Its migrant and seasonal farmworkers, numbering more than 650,000 in California, comprise 44% of the hired agricultural labor in the nation, fueling a $54 billion industry (California Department of Food and Agriculture, 2014). Unfortunately, farmworker families in California do not significantly benefit from that booming picture.

Southern California farmworkers are predominantly Latino, although a smaller subset are African American, Haitian, White, or Asian. And while this population is racially and culturally diverse, 48% of migrant and seasonal farmworkers are U.S. citizens or permanent residents (National Agricultural Worker Survey [NAWS], 2005). Their median annual income is $7,500, and 61% have total family incomes below the poverty level. Local farmworkers struggle with health issues related to their harsh working conditions, such as bone and respiratory problems, allergic reactions, repetitive motion ailments from 12 to 14-hour workdays, exposure to harmful pesticides, and dangerous, unregulated working conditions that often lead to accidents in the fields. Farmworking and mining are the two most dangerous occupations nationally, and serious or fatal accidents are seven times more likely while performing farmwork than in other productive jobs (National Safety Council, 2010). The average life expectancy of migrant and seasonal farmworkers is 49 years of age, in comparison to the U.S. average of 75 years of age (NAWS, 2005). Based on these socioeconomic and labor indicators, it is evident that the life of these invisible neighbors is not easy, and that it involves strong work ethics, dedication to family and community, inner strength, and a will to survive strongly tied to communal solidarity (Jasis & Marriott, 2010).

The Migrant Child

The children of migrant workers struggle to achieve the same level of educational success as their peers. They often do not perform well in school due to a challenging socioeconomic context, and are routinely impacted by poverty, relocation, isolation, and at times, a lack of understanding and flexibility from rigid school cultures. Relocation, particularly if it is a regular occurrence, results in discontinuity in education, which causes migrant students to progress slowly through school and often drop out at a much higher rate than their non-migrant peers. It also negatively affects these students' ability to create and strengthen enduring social relationships and friendships, which, compounded with the cultural and language differences associated with migrant communities, often results in feelings of isolation. Further, migrant students are also at a disadvantage because the majority live in extreme poverty and are compelled to join the workforce in order to contribute to the family's income (González, 2013; Lopez, Scribner, & Mahitivanichcha, 2001). The low socioeconomic indicators of migrant and seasonal farmworker families have a serious impact on their children's health status and living conditions, access to educational, cultural, and recreational opportunities, and their general well-being and readiness to learn.

Migrant Parents and Schools

There is an emerging body of literature studying the role of parent activism in education, its connection to the struggles for social justice in oppressed communities, and its impact on effective and emancipatory pedagogies (Fraga & Frost, 2011; Honig, 2011; Shirley, 2011; Warren and Mapp, 2011). This line of inquiry was originally examined through the decolonizing work of Brazilian pedagogue Paulo Freire (1994), and more recently expanded by Morrell (2008), Rogers and Orr (2011), Warren and Mapp (2011), and Jasis (2013), among others. This area of research analyzes the role of historically underserved communities as they begin to mobilize and challenge oppressive conditions, exploring their particular process of participation, or *grammar of democracy* (Lichtman, 1996), and their potential to impact the direction of educational policy through advocacy and civic engagement (Jasis & Ordoñez-Jasis, 2005).

In the area of migrant education, however, the study of parent activism and inclusive pedagogies is still incipient in its development, in part due to a dominant orientation among researchers towards examining educational experiences in urban settings (Jasis & Marriott, 2010). There are, however, promising new experiences being explored in the context of rural communities, which are expanding this body of literature (Torres, 2014; Zalaquett, Alvarez McHatton & Cranston-Gingras, 2007). For instance, González (2013) provided powerful descriptions of the challenging lives of migrant children workers in a context of poverty and diminished access to schooling. An earlier study by Martinez and Cranston-Gingras (1996) examined the myriad of internal and external challenges faced by migrant students as they struggle to succeed academically in secondary school. They identified nutritional and health problems as critical among migrant children and mobility-induced educational discontinuity as a major cause of distress in the educational lives of migrant students, who because of their lifestyle often start school late and leave early (Zalaquett, Alvarez McHatton, & Cranston-Gingras, 2007). Additionally, educational researchers and practitioners alike point to school personnel misperceptions and negative assumptions about migrant parents, often portraying them as disinterested or neglectful towards their children's schooling (Cranston-Gingras, 2003; Jasis & Marriott, 2010; López et. all, 2001; Torrez, 2014). In fact, as Laureau (1994) suggested, the very meaning of the words "parental involvement," "participation," and the like usually signify different things to different stakeholders in a school community. She argued that many teachers' notions about

54 Pablo Jasis and Alejandro González

parental involvement are narrow, and usually confined to attending parent-teacher conferences, volunteering at classroom activities, fundraising for the school, and helping with homework. Teachers' perceptions are often influenced by the assumption that low-income parents lack the necessary skills to help their children with schoolwork, thus a variety of other possible contributions of working class or minority parents, such as migrant parents, tend to go unnoticed or unrecognized (Auerbach, 2007; Laureau, 1994). As a result, select groups of parents and families with more time and resources end up in a much better position to perform according to the teachers' expectations regarding "parent participation" relative to others (Jasis & Marriott, 2010).

In contrast to these misconceptions, Valdés (1996), Delgado-Gaitán (1994), and Scribner, Young, and Pedroza (1999) have challenged assumptions about working class, Latino families, finding instead a rich source of family values of unity, solidarity, support, and particularly strong views of what constitutes success and failure among these families. And while it is often true that many migrant parents have little information about a school's expectations for their participation, that knowledge gap only adds to the alienation that migrant families often feel at their children's schools (López, 2001; Salinas, 2007).

Along the same lines, Torrez (2014) focused on the need to strengthen bonds of reciprocal understanding between schools and the home culture of migrant families to motivate migrant students towards school success. She argued that administrators and teachers need to better understand bonds of resiliency and strength in the migrant family to create a cultural bridge between schools and homes that will better support student success. Zavala, Pérez, González, and Diaz Villela (2014) concurred, emphasizing the need to engage migrant families in an inclusive, respectful manner with the goal of establishing mutually beneficial connections between families and schools. They explored the pedagogical potential of creating healthier, more inclusive partnerships between migrant families and educational institutions in the context of *respeto* (Valdés, 1996), as a means of promoting access and academic success among migrant students. López et al. (2001) argued that a key factor for the academic success of migrant students is the implementation of well-planned, comprehensive, and inclusive family involvement. In his examination, López et al. (2001) identified a comprehensive list of salient features and policies that create effective partnerships between migrant families and schools, inviting school administrators to allocate significant material as well as non-fungible investments in this relationship. López et al. (2001), González (2013), Salinas (2007), and Danzak (2015) saw the need to create awareness of the most pressing needs of migrant families. They also recommend a sustained commitment to meet those needs to the highest extent possible, establishing ongoing and reciprocal communication with parents, scheduling regular home visits, establishing relational bonds with families (Ramirez, 2010), empowering parents to get involved and be aware of their rights and obligations, involving parents through self-improvement activities, and strengthening collaboration within school programs and with outside agencies.

In spite of a challenging landscape, migrant students and their families continue to view the educational system as a means of social mobility, family, and community empowerment (Jasis & Marriott, 2010; Jasis & Ordoñez-Jasis, 2005). Addressing the challenges to improving migrant student opportunities for school success is becoming more urgent as new generations of migrant families become engaged in a struggle for educational equity and excellence.

Methods and Data Analysis

This study is an ethnographic examination of the narratives of migrant farmworker parents, an exploration of their voices, aspirations, and reflections. The authors explored the issues posed by these migrant community members as participant-observers. Both authors have worked extensively with the migrant community as educators and advocates, which has expanded their knowledge of the participants' context, struggles, and hopes, allowing them to "get a feel for what things mean to the actors" (Weiss, 1998, p. 257). This stance engages the researchers through a capacity to record, describe, and examine behaviors and interactions with proven focus on reliability and relevance, while they are involved in the examined phenomenon within its context and boundaries. As opposed to merely examining an affixed human process and observing its features, this approach engages a social phenomenon as it evolves in context (Weiss, 1998).

This study's ethnographic analysis was informed by Osterling's approach (2001), in which local communities are main sources of valuable assets for their own revitalization and growth. Twelve migrant parents and six teachers of migrant children were interviewed individually and in small focus groups over the span of two months. Their narratives were recorded, transcribed, coded, and organized according to thematic strands (Weiss, 1998). The interviews were conducted in the language of choice of the informants. As a result, most of the conversations with migrant parents were held in Spanish, while interviews with teachers were held in Spanish and English, honoring the participants' choice and level of comfort. The translations were carefully examined for accuracy, cultural specificity, and integrity of meaning, since this study is an exploration of the deeper feelings and understandings of the participants in an effort to "represent the varied interpretations of the multiple actors on the scene" (Weiss, 1998, p. 262), whose reflective process is at the heart of this study.

The intrinsic value of the participants' narratives and the integration of individual and communal stories throughout this study are consistent with the approach to *testimonios* (Beverley, 2005). This approach gives preeminence and center stage to the emerging discourse of historically oppressed

56 Pablo Jasis and Alejandro González

individuals and communities as they challenge their subaltern positioning, understanding their narratives as a way to examine historical junctures and social transformations. Our data analysis was informed by Brunner (1987), who approached narratives as a means to interpret and reinterpret personal experience, in an engagement where narrative and life are seen as profoundly intertwined. Ours is an ethnographic stance guided by the work of Bertaux and Kohli (1984), who understood that personal narratives and reflections contain larger socio-historical complexities and contradictions, in a context where subjectivity plays a central role in human agency. In this context, the term *community* is utilized throughout this study in a dynamic fashion, that is, as a flexible entity which is historically impacted, binding human histories and endeavors through shared interests and struggles, subjectivities, and common visions of society and life.

Findings

It is a warm, dry Southern California morning, and as we wait for the arrival of our interviewees—local, active migrant parents—our conversation alternates between our outrage at the latest attack on immigrant families by a presidential candidate and an update on the health of a teenage migrant student who was injured in a fall at a local high school. The news on the student's status was positive; the local MEP office was able to provide identification and support at the hospital where the teen was transported and his prognosis had improved. That degree of effective and urgent support was not unusual given that the program has established a high level of recognition in the farmworker community. These long-standing relationships with MEP staff allow the program to engage in social action and advocate effectively in support of migrant students and families as they interact with outside institutions. That early morning, we hoped that that level of trust with MEP would allow our parent participants to contribute their memories, hopes, and suggestions as we engaged in learning more about their lives and their relationships to their children's schooling. It was within this context of *convivencia* (Jasis & Jasis Ordoñez, 2005) that we initiated our interactions with local migrant parents, discussing their increased engagement with their children's education. The following sections examine those interactions.

Migrant Parent Voices: Leadership, Motivation, and Commitment

As soon as the six parent participants arrived, we were introduced to each of them, and after sharing handshakes, hugs, and flavorful breakfast burritos, we initiated our interactions. The parents are a couple (mother and father) in their early 40s and four mothers in their 30s. They have varying years of experience collaborating with the local MEP, and although their level of commitment and their motivation for participation are diverse, they all self-identify as "active migrant parents." Leotilda,[1] a mother of three migrant students, told us that "since we are active mothers, the teachers already know us, and then we create the triangle we are looking for: parents, teachers, and students." Nora, a young mother of two, contributed her own experience as an involved migrant parent:

> I am very active in the migrant program, I have grown as a person and as a mom, and my self-esteem has increased, especially now that I have a child with special needs and the services we fight for are very important.

We can feel an undercurrent of pride and assertiveness in their voices when these parents speak of their participation and belonging in MEP. There is also overt frustration towards less active parents. María, a mother of three, shares those feelings at our meeting, "I get angry with the moms and dads who don't go to the migrant meetings. You learn a lot in these meetings! We need to learn to make the best of the help we get." Alexa, a young mother of two with an easy demeanor and a wide smile, believes that there is much more to participating than attending MEP meetings. She connects her participation as an active migrant parent to her valuable quest towards self-actualization; in her words:

> Of course my main motivation to participate in the program are my children and my family, but I also do it for myself because I want them to follow my example! That's why I am now studying to obtain my GED and get ready for my job training. In reality, we are the change!

Juan, a migrant father of three who, together with his wife Viviana, has taken various leadership roles in MEP in the last few years, contributes his own reflection:

> I fight because I learned it from my parents, and my motivation is the community. I enjoy representing the program, because that participation helps us grow, I don't think we should have any limits to participate or to support our children.

Viviana supports her husband's assertions, and adds a comment that aptly describes her leadership role in the migrant community: "I love being of service to people, and that's something that you learn at the migrant parents' conferences!" Nelly, a young mother who takes turns between contributing to the conversation and looking after her two young children in an adjacent room, adds the following comment: "I believe that in the migrant program all parents have a common goal: to see our children as accomplished individuals, *es que en la familia está nuestra fuerza* (our family is our strength)!"

Another gathering of active MEP parents interviewed the following week echoed the reflections of this group of migrant parents. This time, our

58   *Pablo Jasis and Alejandro González*

meeting was held at a high school in a small town located at the heart of agricultural production in a coastal Southern California community. This town is surrounded by productive fields where farmwork is the mainstay of economic life. Four mothers and two fathers are the farmworker participants, all of them proud and active migrant parents at the local and regional level. Ismael, a young father of two, who came to the meeting with his wife Esther, shared his first impressions as a migrant:

> I came to this country when I was 15 years old to work in the orange fields. We were 10 people living in a small apartment where there were several children, all crowded. Then I asked myself what are these kids' chances of doing well in school?

Ismael's wife, Esther, shared her motivation to be active in the migrant program:

> As a female I could not study when I was younger, and that was especially bad for young girls. But now, the vision of my generation is very different, it is a vision of university education for our children, and for that we have to be active.

Ismael has meaningful words about his work as a migrant parent representative and the importance of his parent activism. He stated:

> I realized that us, migrant parents, we have power, but we are a sleeping power, because if we don't use that power it just stays there. It is of no use to blame parents who don't participate, the questions we should ask ourselves are, "How can I help my children? How can I attract more parents to the program?"

Migrant Parent Views on Struggle and Partnerships

Much of the conversations with the migrant parents explored their visions of community pride and struggle. Ismael, a migrant parent leader, shares with the group his reflection about the meaning of being a migrant farmworker:

> Some people believe that "being migrant" is something ugly, something inferior. In truth, being a migrant is a synonym of struggle. We are all migrants in this life, and I say it with pride!

Seeing activism and life itself as a process of struggle is a common theme among these migrant parents. It is a struggle that deepens their commitment towards the improvement of living conditions and a hopeful future for the community. Mr. Beraja, a veteran migrant worker and father of two daughters in the program, emphasizes this point and transforms it into an intergenerational message: "My parents didn't know how to read or write, that's why I don't want my daughters going through what I went through. I want them to graduate from college so they can help the community."

The parents' disposition towards the local migrant community's emerging assertiveness is also present in the group's conversations and mirrored in their increasingly empowered relationships with their children's teachers. Nelly, a young migrant mother, also contributes to this point: "my relationship with my children's teachers is very positive now, though it was a little competitive before, and being active in MEP helped me with that."

The development of stronger partnerships with migrant parents is also a priority for their most committed teachers. Mariana Díaz, a resource teacher at a local middle school, is well aware of the need to strengthen the collaboration with the migrant community. She describes her interactions with migrant parents in the following terms: "I have strong relationships with migrant families, now they are very open with me, they are not afraid to talk to me, and having that openness is very important!" Javier Prado, Steve Garcia, and Martin Solórzano are all teachers at a local high school who routinely collaborate with the migrant program. Many of their students come from migrant families or are migrant farmworkers themselves, and their experience strengthens their determination to partner with the children's families. Javier comments that "migrant parents want their kids to succeed, but if the communication goes through the kids, it is just not enough; it doesn't work . . . we need new strategies to reach out to these families." Steve has an assessment of his own regarding the need to connect with migrant families:

> We need more communication with the families, we need to be informed about PTA or parent council meetings, so we can communicate the information to migrant families. When we plan activities for migrant families we need to provide transportation, since many of the families live in far away areas, or maybe it would be better to take the activities where they live. Transportation is a big deal around here.

Martin adds the shared belief among these teachers that migrant families are seriously invested in their children's schooling, and that teachers have a critical role in enhancing their chances for success: "I know they want to support their kids, but at times they don't know how! To me the main issue is to start earlier talking about expectations, and provide the specific services that are individual to each of their kids!"

Developing a Sense of Hope

Some of the migrant parents who participated in this study represent a leading sector of a much larger community. They shared a history of consciousness raising (Freire, 1994), various levels of organizing experience

60 Pablo Jasis and Alejandro González

after having developed strong views of the strengths, needs, and desires of migrant families, and a hopeful vision that fuels their sustained activism. Juan, a leading parent activist, summarizes his approach to the migrant community's future with these words: "I see a different future for us, I see more positivity with the people who are in this struggle, sometimes we are only five or six in our meetings, but there are going to be many more of us!"

In our meetings with migrant families and educators—and often against a backdrop of dire social and economic challenges—there was a palpable feeling of possibility and hope towards better educational and life opportunities for their children and for themselves. Freire (2014) describe this disposition as "the foundation of hope," a stance that requires us to "work on the question of hope, to increase hope, hope in spite of it all. Because without hope there can be no struggle" (p. 51). That sense of hope and possibility is an undercurrent that impacts all migrant parent activities, organizing events, and family dynamics that we observed. It is a foundation for what with Freire, Freire, and Oliveira (2014) call a *pedagogy of solidarity*, which in this context becomes a community-based and generational phenomenon, as depicted in the description of Viviana, the migrant activist mother, who believes that a shared sense of solidarity and service to her peers also begins to appear in her family.

> I noticed that my oldest daughter, who is only 11, is leading and supporting her younger siblings when it comes to schoolwork. She makes them feel safe, she plans their studies and presentations with them at home about many things, and she follows what we tell each other during our migrant activities "*hay que compartir lo que uno sabe (we have to share what one knows)!*"

A strong component of the migrant parents' participation in the program and at their children's schools is their increasing representation at the local, regional, and state levels, which has developed their sense of leadership and helped familiarize them with their rights and responsibilities. It is what Lichtman (1996) calls the community's *grammar of democracy*, that is, the particular ways of effective participation that involve a sense of shared commitment, pragmatism, and efficacy in advocating for migrant children. Nelly, a young migrant mother, asserts this with her comments.

> I say to my *compañeras* the same thing I tell my children: we are a team in which we share everything, we do our part and they do theirs. We are a team and that way we form our character, and that's the way we move forward too!

Her approach is closely related to Worgs' (2011) notion of *co-production* in the educational arena, which he describes as an effort by community members to develop "the will and the capacity to try to narrow the gap

Strengths of Migrant Families   61

between what is desired and what the state has provided" (p. 89). Through this process, migrant parents are building together the necessary skills to extend what is offered by MEP and share it with their peers, maximizing opportunities for all their children.

Bonds of Strength and Solidarity

The strengths of migrant families lie in their ability to strengthen their bonds of solidarity and their intrinsic motivation. Robert Bellah (1985) articulated the concept of *community of memory*, which he describes as:

> tying us to the past but also turning us toward the future as communities of hope. They carry a context of meaning that can allow us to connect our aspirations for ourselves and those closest to us with the aspirations of a larger whole and see our own efforts as being, in part, contributions to a common good.
>
> (p. 153)

The memories of these migrant parents fuel their motivations, their frustrations, and triumphs, as Nelly, a young farmworker mother and active MEP participant, explains:

> When I was a young child my dream was to become a teacher someday, but once you get married and begin to work hard, those dreams become more and more difficult, because you also need to take care of your home . . . but I know it will be different for my daughters because I am so involved.

Her sister María, also a farmworker mother, nods as she listens to Nelly's reflections, and adds the following comment:

> My motivations for involving myself in migrant activities have evolved. First I joined because I felt isolated, but now I really want to leave an impact on the people! We all want to be role models for our children and tell them: You all are going to achieve as much as you want in your lives!

In line with the recommendations of Torrez (2014) and Lopez, Scribner, and Mahitivanichcha (2001), these parent activists believe in strong partnerships with their children's teachers to improve schooling for migrant students. The partnership they pose to schools is through an empowerment approach (Jasis & Ordoñez-Jasis, 2005), that is, through a process where individuals, organizations, and communities gain *mastery* over their lives (Rappaport, 1984). In this context, active migrant families strive to connect with teachers and school personnel through a more balanced relationship,

62   Pablo Jasis and Alejandro González

in which all sides contribute to benefit the students. Mr. Beraja, a migrant parent, shared his experience with these words:

> Every day we ask our kids, "how is your teacher talking to you? Are you learning? What did you learn today?" And some of the same questions we need to ask from the teachers, we need to be involved all the time and always communicate with teachers. They need to know we are here for them too!

Migrant Parents as Education Advocates

Throughout our meetings with these migrant parents, the interviews with their children's teachers, as well as observations of their organizing and learning activities, many informants shared deeply felt lessons in resiliency, a restored sense of hope for a better future, and an ongoing commitment to community and family values of solidarity and inner strength. We found that the migrant parents were generally aware that there are programs and activities that can benefit their children at school, but that only their active participation and advocacy at school will make those activities and programs available to their families. These parents also know that their individual and collective effort is critical in ensuring that other migrant parents receive the information they need to support their own children, thus, they see themselves as organizing and educating agents for the migrant community at large.

Generally, migrant parents believe that the MEP and its local representatives are their main source of training and networking for information and organizing opportunities, and that the program staff has the best interests of their children at heart. All parents interviewed emphasized the need for families to better connect and participate in their children's schools, but they also understood the socioeconomic pressures impacting farmworker parents and the limited opportunities many of them have to become more active in their schools and communities. As a result, they consider themselves as the emerging voices of a larger community with many informational needs, believing that the migrant community has the potential to advocate for migrant interests and for changes that can benefit their children.

Our process of interviewing migrant parent activists and their children's teachers also suggests that both participant groups envisioned a stronger partnership and greater communication with each other as the key to migrant student success. These parents believed that all teachers needed to be more aware of the pressures farmworker families endure, but also to recognize their family-based resilience and their hope in a better educational future for their children. For their part, the teachers interviewed for this study wanted better communication with school and district administrators about the needs of migrant students. They also believed that there is a need to establish better communication with the migrant program and its representatives to identify and assess migrant students as early as possible to better serve these children. According to them, individual assessments of migrant students should not be limited to academic and linguistic needs, but also include nutritional, medical, visual, dental, counseling, and even housing, transportation, and other socioeconomic and cultural indicators. They believed that schools must take a critical role in connecting migrant families to community-based services, with the dual goal of meeting the urgent needs of the families and to create a stronger foundation of trust with the school.

Parents and teachers agreed that a major institutional investment to improve educational services for migrant children is needed in schools and districts serving farmworker families (López et al., 2001). The educational investment these critical stakeholders envisioned went beyond funds—which are also clearly needed to support stronger services—and include a concerted and mutual quest for advocacy, community education, leadership training, and joint action to achieve the "feasible, visible results" (Jasis & Ordoñez-Jasis, 2005) that can have a lasting impact on the education of migrant students.

Implications and Conclusion

Schools impacted by large numbers of migrant children need to maximize their opportunities to collaborate with migrant parents, beginning with a serious effort to identify them and their needs, and then be eligible for additional support by the MEP. Secondly, schools need to identify the community's strengths and challenges, and thus invest the necessary resources and training to partner effectively with the migrant community. Logistical support, such as transportation to meetings and events, translation of documents and announcements, as well as childcare and taking school activities directly to migrant communities if they are distant from the school campus, are all essential to family participation. It is also important to create opportunities for self-governance and self-expression for farmworker families, whose socio-cultural and economic contexts are often markedly different from those of other students and families. The hiring of community advocates who themselves are from a migrant background would be a significant step to bridge an effective communication with migrant families. Of equal importance is the relationship between local MEP agencies and the community-based organizations that focus on supporting the educational, social, and health needs of migrant families.

As we have seen from the migrant parents' narratives, their energy and commitment towards the educational success of their children are well-documented and remain strong. Their sense of solidarity and efforts towards developing leadership in their community are also palpable and ongoing. We are certain that these dispositions will help support stronger and more durable partnerships with the schools their children attend. In this context, the words

64 Pablo Jasis and Alejandro González

of Arnove (2009), who said that "education will continue to be a critical battlefield where people imagine and fight for an alternative present and future" (p. 89), become particularly appropriate for migrant families. The increasingly strong parents of the migrant community continue fighting and advocating to keep that struggle alive.

Note

1 All names are pseudonyms.

References

Arnove, A. (2009). Education and social justice movements. In W. Ayers, T. Quinn and D. Stovall (Eds.), *Handbook of social justice in education* (pp. 88–89). New York and London: Routledge.

Auerbach, S. (2007). From moral supporters to struggling advocates: Reconceptualizing parent roles in education through the experience of working-class families of color. *Urban Education, 42*(3), 250–283.

Bellah, R. (1985). *Habits of the heart: Individualism and commitment in American life.* Oakland: University of California Press.

Bertaux, D. & Kohli, M. (1984). The life story approach: A continental view. *Annual Review of Sociology, 10,* 215–237.

Beverley, J. (2005). Testimonio, subalternity and narrative authority. In N. Denzin & Y. Lincoln (Eds.), *The SAGE handbook of qualitative research* (pp. 547–559). Thousand Oaks, CA: Sage.Brunner, Jerome. (1987). Life as narrative. *Social Research, 54*(1): 11–32.

California Department of Food and Agriculture. (2014). California agricultural production statistics. Retrieved on June 1, 2016 from https://www.cdfa.ca.gov/statistics/

Chávez, L. (1982). *Shadowed lives: Undocumented immigrants in American society.* San Diego, CA: Harcourt Brace.

Cranston-Gingras, A. (2003). Reconnecting youth from migrant farmworker families. *Reclaiming Children and Youth, 11*(4), 242–246.

Cruickshank, B. (1999). *The will to empower: Democratic citizens and other subjects.* Ithaca, NY: Cornell University Press.

Danzak, R. L. (2015). The meaning of roots: How a migrant farmworker student developed a bilingual-bicultural identity through change. *Global Education Review, 2*(2), 24–42.

Delgado-Gaitan, C. (1994). Sociocultural change through literacy: Toward the empowerment of families. In B. M. Ferdman, R. M. Weber, & A. G. Ramírez (Eds.), *Literacy across languages and cultures* (pp. 143–169). New York: State University of New York Press.

Fraga, L. & Frost, A. (2011). Democratic institutions, public engagement, and Latinos in American public schools. In M. Orr & J. Rogers (Eds.), *Public engagement for public education* (pp.117–139). Redwood City, CA: Stanford University Press.

Freire, P. (1994). *Pedagogy of hope: Reliving pedagogy of the oppressed.* New York: Continuum Press.

Freire, P. (2014). *Pedagogy of solidarity.* Walnut Creek, CA: Left Coast Press.

Freire, P., Araujo Freire, A. & De Oliveira, W. (2014). *Pedagogy of Solidarity.* Walnut Creek, CA: Left Coast Press.

González, A. (2013). *Latino migrant parent influence on Latino migrant student university enrollment*. (Unpublished Doctoral dissertation). California State University Fullerton, Fullerton, CA.

Gonzalez, G. (1994). *Labor and community: Mexican citrus worker villages in a Southern California county*. Champaign: University of Illinois Press.

Henig, J. (2011). The contemporary context of public engagement: The new political grid. In M. Orr & J. Rogers (Eds.), *Public engagement for public education* (pp. 52–89). Redwood City, CA: Stanford University Press.

Jasis, P. (2013). Latino families challenging exclusion in a middle school: A story from the trenches. *The School Community Journal, 23*(1), 111–130.

Jasis, P. & Marriott, D. (2010). *Todo por nuestros hijos*/All for our children: Migrant families and parent participation at an alternative education program. *Journal of Latinos in Education, 9*(2), 126–140.

Jasis, P. & Ordoñez-Jasis, R. (2005). Convivencia to empowerment: Latino parent organizing at la familia. *The High School Journal, 88*(2), 33–42.

Lareau, A. (1994). Parent involvement in schooling: A dissenting view. In C. Fagnano & B. Werber (Eds.), *School, family and community interaction: A view from the firing lines* (pp. 61–73). San Francisco, CA: Westview Press.

Lichtermann, P. (1996). *The search for political community: American activists reinventing commitment*. Cambridge, MA: Cambridge University Press.

Lopez, G. R., Scribner, J. D. & Mahitivanichcha, K. (2001). Redefining parental involvement: Lessons from high-performing migrant-impacted schools. *American Educational Research Journal, 38*(2), 253–288.

Martinez, Y. G. & Cranston-Gingras, A. (1996). Migrant farmworker students and the educational process: Barriers to high school completion. *The High School Journal, 80*(1), 28–38.

Morrell, E (2008). *Critical Literacy and Urban Youth: Pedagogies of Access, Dissent, and Liberation*. New York & London: Routledge.

Moynihan, D. (1969). *On understanding poverty: Perspectives from the social sciences*. New York: Basic Books.

National Agricultural Worker Survey. (2005). U.S. department of labor. Retrieved from http://www.doleta.gov/agworker/naws.cfm

National Safety Council. (2010). Stats services, most dangerous occupations. Retrieved from http://www.nsc.org/news_resources/Resources/res_stats_services/Pages/FrequentlyAskedQuestions.aspx#question5

Osterling, J. (2001). Waking the sleeping giant: Engaging and capitalizing on the strengths of the Latino community. *Bilingual Research Journal, 25*(2), 59–88.

Ramirez, D. (2010). Building family support for student achievement: CABE Project INSPIRE Parent Leadership Development Program. *Multilingual Educator*. Conference Edition, California Association of Bilingual Education.

Rappaport, J. (1984). Studies in empowerment: Introduction to the issues. In J. Rappaport, C. Swift & R. Hess (Eds.), *Studies in empowerment: Steps toward understanding and action* (pp. 1–7). New York: The Haworth Press.

Rogers, J. & Orr, M. (2011). *Public engagement for public education: Joining forces to revitalize democracy and equalize schools*. Redwood City, CA: Stanford University Press.

Romanowsky, M. H. (2003). Meeting the unique needs of the children of migrant farmworkers. *Wilson Web Clearing House, 77*(1), 27–33.

66 Pablo Jasis and Alejandro González

Salinas, J. (2007). *Educational experiences of children in the migrant stream: Ecological factors necessary for academic success.* (Unpublished dissertation). Bowling Green, OH: Bowling Green State University.

Scribner, J., Young, M. & Pedroza, A. (1999). Building collaborative relations with parents. In P. Reyes, J. Scribner & A. Paredes (Eds.), *Lessons from high performing Hispanic schools: Creating learning communities* (pp. 36–60). New York, NY: Teachers College Press.

Shirley, D. (2011). A brief history of public engagement in American education. In M. Orr & J. Rogers (Eds.), *Public engagement for public education* (pp. 27–52). Redwood City, CA: Stanford University Press.

Torrez, J. (2014). "Teachers should be like us!" bridging migrant communities to rural Michigan classrooms. *Multicultural Education, 21*(3–4), 39–44.

Valdés, G. (1996). *Con respeto: Bridging the differences between culturally diverse families and schools.* New York: Teachers College Press.

Warren, M. & Mapp, K. (2011). *A match on dry grass: Community organizing as a catalyst for school reform.* New York: Oxford University Press.

Weiss, C. (1998). *Evaluation: Methods for studying programs and policies.* Upper Saddle, NJ: Prentice Hall.

Worgs, D. (2011). Public engagement and the coproduction of public education. In M. Orr & J. Rogers (Eds.), *Public engagement for public education* (pp. 89–116). Redwood City, CA: Stanford University Press.

Zalaquett, C., Alvarez McHatton, P. & Cranston-Gingras, A. (2007). Characteristics of Latina/o migrant farmworker students attending a large metropolitan university. *Journal of Hispanic Higher Education, 6*(2), 135–156.

Zavala, M., Pérez, P., González, A. & Díaz Villela, A. (2014). Con respeto: A conceptual model for building healthy community-university partnerships alongside Mexican migrant families. *Journal of Critical Thought and Praxis, 3*(2). Retrieved from http://lib.dr.iastate.edu/jctp/vol3/iss2/5

5 Designing Programs to Meet and Assess the Needs of Migrant Students

Fernando Rodríguez-Valls and Sandra Kofford

Every year in California, Migrant Program Offices within the County Offices of Education file their Regional Applications (RA) in order to apply for the federal funding allocated and administered by the Migrant Education Office (MEO) at the California Department of Education (CDE). School districts across the U.S. that are implementing programs and providing services to migrant students and their families follow the same compliance. All school districts, whether MEO directly funds them or they work within the county offices of education, have to file a District Service Agreement (DSA). Both RAs and DSAs must include a detailed description—number of students participating, timelines, goals, objectives, measurable outcomes, assessment tools, and budget—of all programs and services the county office and/or school districts will implement during the next fiscal year.

These programs and services are divided into seven support areas with specific goals: 1) School Readiness: prepare preschool students ages two to five years old and their parents for compulsory education systems; 2) Language Arts: support migrant students in the development and acquisition of language skills in both their native languages (e.g., Mixteco, Zapoteco, Triqui, Nahuatl, and Spanish) and English; 3) Mathematics: strengthen and increase the academic performance of PK-12 migrant students; 4) High School: increase graduation rates for migrant students; 5) Out-of-School Youth (OSY): provide guidance and opportunities for the here-to-work migrant population to obtain their General Education Diploma (GED) and to increase their professional skills; 6) Health: offer dental and optometry services as well as develop programs to proactively prevent migrant families from exposure to pesticides, chemicals, and other hazards related to their work in the fields and slaughterhouses; and 7) Parent Involvement: inform, educate, and empower parents to actively participate in their children's education and to become advocates for an equitable and high quality education. It is important to notice that all these services are supplemental; thus, they cannot replace additional support services migrant students should receive, such as Title I. Further, educational programs must be offered either before school, after school, on Saturday, and/or during the summer. The premise is that migrant students are not to be pulled out of the classroom for

68 *Fernando Rodríguez-Valls and Sandra Kofford*

these services. They must be part of and contribute with their non-migrant peers to the same instructional and educational opportunities (Educational Code- 54442(a)).

Our experience[1] has taught us that most of the programs identified in each one of these seven aforesaid areas, as they are depicted and narrated in the RAs and DSAs, include programs that have been originally designed for other at-risk students, such as English Learners, low-income students, and/or immigrant students. Though these labels may apply to a large number of migrant students, the reality is that migrant students have specific needs that must be understood, identified, addressed, and included in all the supplemental programs designed by educational agencies working with migrant students and their families. Further, personnel designing these programs must take into consideration how mobility and anonymization impact migrant students' learning practices and lifestyles (Rodríguez-Valls & Torres, 2014). It is pivotal, in terms of effectiveness and sustainability, that county offices and school districts develop fully inclusive programs in which migrant students receive the appropriate services as defined in their Individual Learning Plans (ILP).

Migrant families are by definition mobile and face many challenges when moving to a new city or to a new state. Lack of belonging and anonymization are among some of the struggles migrant students face when arriving at a new school. Prewitt-Diaz, Trotter, and Rivera's (1990) ethnographic study on migrant families describes this lack of belonging: "It's hard to always leave and say goodbye all the time" (p. 48), and add, "Migrants [often] talked about isolation and constant adjustment to new surroundings" (p. 59). In another ethnographic study, Lu and Zhou (2013), when analyzing similar traits in migrant students in China, state, "It would be fruitful to implement social programs that bolster migrant children's sense of belonging and raise urbanites' acceptance of migrants" (p. 114).

A 2008 report written on education and migration by the Network of Experts in Social Sciences of Education and training (NESSE) highlights the importance of supporting the construction of social capital by migrant families. The report underlines that "social capital tends to consist mostly of relations within the ethnic group that has migrated" (p. 31). Thus, it is crucial that educational agencies design programs that focus on the specific needs of the migrant children, and educate and empower migrant parents with tools on how to belong, navigate the U.S. educational system, and the intricacies and nuances of their communities (Quezada, Rodríguez-Valls, & Lindsey, this volume; Quezada, Rodríguez-Valls, & Lindsey, 2016).

The lack of belonging often carries a sentiment of anonymization among migrant students and their families (Rodríguez-Valls & Torres, 2014). Anonymization is a two-layer barrier. The first level is the bureaucratic anonymization that prevents thousands of migrant students from receiving services as soon as they arrive at a new school site.

The Migrant Education Office (MEO) in the California Department of Education (CDE) created the Migrant Student Information Network (MSIN) to gather student data and to expedite the identification of migrant students when they are making qualifying moves. Aligned with this effort, the Office of Migrant Education (OME) in the U.S. Department of Education built the Migrant Student Records Exchange Initiative (MSIX) to support the state networks. Despite the support of systems like MSIN at the state level in California and MSIX[2] at the national level, students are not identified soon enough; hence, they are not participating in programs nor opting to receive services that could ease their adaptation to a new community. To prevent these lapses of support, Migrant Education programs must include tools that underline the importance of being preemptive when looking for support rather than waiting for the services and programs (Valdés, 2003).

The second layer of anonymization comes when the curriculum implemented in the schools lacks connections with the linguistic and cultural wealth migrant families bring to the learning processes (Moll, Amanti, Neff, & Gonzalez, 1992; Valenzuela, 1999, 2016). Without explicit links with the history, concepts, and texts analyzed in the classroom, the migrant student tends to deny their migrant status, as this carries a negative connotation. This connotation draws from deficit approaches when defining and portraying migrant and immigrant families (Barlett & García, 2011; Nieto, 2013; Thorpe, 2011).

In the next section, we will outline the key characteristics exemplary migrant education must include. Short-term effectiveness must integrate the student into the school rather than asking her or him to assimilate. Further, the long-term impact must equip students with tools that value and enhance their identity as migrant students who critically think, create, and deeply know; therefore, she or he will not be afraid to move (Rodríguez-Izquierdo, 2015).

Key Elements in Exemplary Migrant Programs

Before examining exemplary practices, we will relay the key elements and responsibilities that must be included in any migrant education program. According to the 34 Code of Federal Regulations (CFR) 200.83(a),[3] "An SEA (State Educational Agency) that receives a grant of MEP funds must develop and update a written comprehensive State plan based on a current statewide needs assessment." The SEA must include in the State Service Delivery Plan (SSDP) at least the following five components: 1) Performance Targets, 2) Needs Assessment, 3) Measurable Program Outcomes, 4) Service Delivery, and 5) Evaluation. The SEA must consult with the State Parent Advisory Council (SPAC) when developing the SSDP. Moreover, the SEA must ensure that all Local Educational Agencies (LEAs) that receive funding to implement supplemental Migrant Education programs are in compliance and follow the guidelines and recommendations comprised in the SSDP.

State Educational Agencies across the country, in conjunction with LEAs—County Offices and School Districts—develop both the SSDP and the Comprehensive Needs Assessment (CNA). The design and development of these two documents follows five steps (See Figure 5.1). First, LEAs conduct a CNA to evaluate the effectiveness and the quality of their programs in the seven areas described above (e.g., School Readiness, Parent Involvement, etc.). The goal of the CNA is to outline the needs of both migrant students and parents. With all the CNAs completed by the LEAs, the SEA begins to design the SSDP, the purpose of which is to provide guidance to all LEAs with the target goal of supporting migrant students and their families to overcome the challenges they face due to their high mobility. Moreover, the SSDP specifies the goals, objectives, and outcomes that need to be included in the programs described in both the RA and DSA. These goals, objectives, and outcomes are intended to warrant that all migrant students receive the support needed to achieve high academic standards; parents are informed and educated to be actively and effectively involved in their children's education. With the framework and guidance provided by the SSDP, LEAs begin the implementation of the programs explained in their RAs and DSAs. As they implement the programs, LEAs collect data and evaluate this data to prepare them for the next CNA, which ideally is written every three to five years.

Though the regulations (CFR 34) are clear on the steps to follow and the elements that need to be included in these documents, oftentimes, LEAs have difficulty in designing programs that meet the specific needs highlighted in the SSDP.

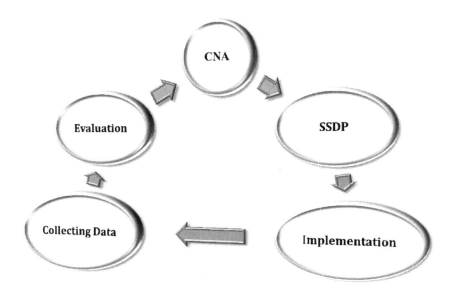

Figure 5.1 Development and Design of SSDP and CNA

Our experiences on both sides of the spectrum, both designing programs and evaluating RAs and DSAs, have taught us that the best programs and services in migrant education are the ones which include these four components:

1 Have observable, measurable, and assessable goals aligned with the Individual Learning Plans (ILP), the Comprehensive Needs Assessment (CNA), and the State Service Delivery Plan (SSDP).
2 Promote and implement multilingual and multicultural education through cultural and linguistic pedagogies.
3 Use the funds of knowledge of migrant families.
4 Target both students and parents.

The alignment between programs and services, ILPs, CNAs, and SSDP is crucial when developing a continuum that supports and meets the needs of migrant students and their families. Without specific goals, objectives, and outcomes, programs lack efficacy and effectiveness (Echeverría, Vogt, & Short, 2013). The ILPs identify specific needs when students arrive in a new school district. Personnel designing migrant programs must examine how these specifics correlate to the areas identified in CNAs and SSDPs. This analysis is crucial to avoid the placement of migrant students in programs that lack both the specificity and the differentiation needed to reach high levels of academic performance.

Migrant students and their families, as explained previously, carry a linguistic and cultural richness educators could use to enrich their practices (Delpit, 2006; Luke, 2013). As Quezada, Rodríguez-Valls, and Lindsey (2016) explain, personnel working in migrant programs must be culturally proficient if they aim to avoid practices that either suppress, ignore, or deny the lack of belonging and anonymization migrant students and their families may experience when arriving in a new community. As topics to be discussed when designing effective supplemental practices, personnel working in migrant programs should acknowledge, learn, and optimally, include the cultural and linguistic richness migrant students and their families bring when arriving in a new community.

Further, migrant programs and services are to consider migrant students and their families as knowledgeable others capable of supporting, enhancing, and enriching teaching and learning processes (Moll, 2013). When defining best practices, Gay (2010) describes how "teachers must learn how to recognize, honor, and incorporate the personal abilities of students into their teaching strategies. If this is done, then school [migrant students'] achievement will improve" (p. 1).

Recognizing, honoring, and incorporating personal abilities must refer to both students and parents. The uniqueness of the Migrant Education Program is that it is a family program targeting both parents and students. When developing and enhancing language and literacy skills, the programs' goals, objectives, and outcomes must reflect cooperative learning experiences in which parents and students learn how to negotiate mainstream and oppressing literacies (Freire & Macedo, 1987; Vasquez, 2004). The final goal is to educate the new generation of self-sufficient migrant students and families who can successfully navigate compulsory education systems, as well as to equip them with tools that would allow them to question the status quo and to educate those who judge them because of their migrant status.

What follows are two examples of best practices in Migrant Education. These two programs typify high-quality, well-designed, and research-based programs in an era of globalization, where migratory flows are constantly changing demographics and identities (Žižek, 2013).

Best Practices in Migrant Education

Family Biliteracy Program

Following the guidelines provided by the Office of Migrant Education (OME) in the U.S. Department of Education, migrant programs targeting students ages two to five years old should be designed to[4] "help break the cycle of poverty and improve the literacy of participating migrant families by integrating early childhood education, adult literacy or adult basic education, and parenting education into a unified family literacy program." Although the federal program Migrant Even Start, designed to support migrant students ages two to five years old, has almost been dismantled, all the states are still committed to providing services in early childhood education to migrant children and their families. Aligned with this commitment to increase the levels of [bi]literacy of migrant students and their families, a group of educators created Family Biliteracy "to provide the space . . . for parents to value their literacy skills as an educational asset, and . . . [for] students to become biliterate and global students" (Rodríguez-Valls, Montoya, & Valenzuela, 2014, p. 108).

As mentioned before, the majority of programs described in the RAs and DSAs from county offices and school districts in California include programs that were designed for student populations such as English Learner (EL) students. Further, programs tend to focus on the idea of mastering English rather than promoting, supporting, and valuing biliteracy as an asset for migrant students and their families. Piller (2016), in her analysis of language and equality in migrant populations, poses two important questions: "How does linguistic proficiency mediate social participation? In short, how is language related to inequality?" (p. 2).

Reformulating these questions, the authors asked themselves: why are migrant students being educated to become monolingual in English when many of their counterparts—native speakers in English—are working to increase their language proficiency in a second language? And, what evidence backs the idea of using monolingual approaches when expanding the acquisition and learning of English of migrant students who already have competency in their home language–Mixteco, Zapoteco, Triqui, and/or Spanish?

Moving away from deficit approaches that colonize and oppress the migrant population, the Family Biliteracy Program reinforces students' native language as an asset to scaffold the learning of L2 but most importantly reinstalls the basic principles of linguistic social justice (Lippi-Green, 2011). Teaching migrant students and their families the importance of maintaining and augmenting their home language skills as they acquire English is a proactive methodology to meet various goals highlighted in the last SSDP conducted in 2010[5] by the Migrant Education Office at CDE: a) to ensure migrant students enter kindergarten at the same average age as non-migrant students; and b) to increase the graduation rate of migrant students as compared with non-migrant students.

To accomplish both goals, Family Biliteracy stresses the importance of increasing the number of vocabulary words migrant students know, use, and comprehend in their home before they enter kindergarten. Various studies explain the positive impact of high levels of literacy in their home language when acquiring a second language (Escamilla, Hopewell, & Butvilofsky, 2013; García, 2009; García & Kleifgen, 2010; Rodríguez, Carrasquillo, & Soon Lee, 2014).

By reinforcing their home language, Family Biliteracy tackles another important problem, the number of Long Term English Learners (LTEL) among the migrant population. Laurie Olsen (2010), in her analysis of LTELs, underlines a common factor identifying the majority of LETLs: "there is evidence from studies of students' cumulative files and personal histories that Long Term English Learners were not in programs that developed their home language" (p. 17).

Family Biliteracy creates opportunities for both students and parents to increase their levels of literacy in their first language as well as in English. Moreover, it fosters the development of their home language by students and parents working together during the whole program. This feature is unique because the majority of migrant early childhood programs described in RAs and DSAs have parents and students working separately. In contrast, parents in this program receive training on how to support language development at home while their children are working with teachers on foundations of literacy.

Having parents and students working together at all times maximizes and optimizes the activities implemented by teachers. Together, students and parents learn how to face and overcome the challenges embedded in language acquisition processes. Further, having them together strengthens the idea that a family that reads, writes, listens, speaks, and comprehends together grows as a unified multilingual, multicultural, responsive, and inclusive family (Trujillo Sáez, Lorenzo, & Vez, 2011; Shin, 2012).

74 Fernando Rodríguez-Valls and Sandra Kofford

Currently, the Family Biliteracy Program is implemented statewide in California. The Migrant Education Office allocates $500,000 each year to award 10 grants of $50,000 each "to promote . . . family biliteracy programs . . . that focus on the academic, language, social, and cross-cultural challenges of school, [and] will better prepare at-risk migrant children for entrance into kindergarten."[6] In academic year 2014–2015, the Migrant Education Office at the Idaho Department of Education piloted the Family Biliteracy Program following a home-based approach.[7] Paraprofessionals visited the students' homes on a weekly basis to work with the whole family developing literacy skills in their home language and their second language. In both states, the preliminary outcomes have shown a positive effect in how teachers prepare themselves to design practices that endorse and underpin biliteracy, how parents perceive and value biliteracy as an asset, and how students enter kindergarten seeing their home language as an academic tool rather than a stigma and a deficit (Martín Peris, 2010; Paffey, 2014).

Language Explorers

For older students, it is perhaps even more important to fully engage them in reading, writing, speaking, and listening in an atmosphere that honors their identity and builds upon their existing funds of knowledge (Moll, Amanti, Neff, & Gonzalez, 1992). Language Explorers was created for migrant students and enriched with feedback provided by teachers and students. This curriculum transformed how educators working with migrant students and their families participated in the educational system. Instead of duplicating or adapting a program designed for other groups of students (e.g., immigrants, ELs), Language Explorers opened a path for migrant education to become a producer of best practices rather than just the "beneficiary" of other practices.

Language Explorers is a four-week curriculum implemented during summer school and after-school supplemental programs. In these programs, students read, deconstruct, and analyze multimodal stories: Tupac Shakur's poems (1999), Sandra Cisneros' vignettes (1991), Gary Soto's poetry (2006), and Gene Luen Yang's graphic novels (2008). These texts are augmented with videos, photos, art, and music; thus, students have various venues to share their understanding and to pose questions. The written text is the beginning and the ending point in a journey defined as an "intellectual commute" (Rodríguez-Valls, Kofford, & Morales, 2012). Students walk through the intellectual commute by first reading a text, listening to a song, or watching a video; then they draw a response showing their understanding of the piece analyzed, and later use this visual to support their written response, which will be compared and contrasted with the original piece—text, song, or video.

The main goals of this intellectual commute are: a) to experiment with different forms of expression; b) to own their work; and c) to empower migrant students. On a more concrete level, the objectives are for students to: critically evaluate the experiences and the messages depicted in the written texts and in other media (music, graffiti, videos); create their own understanding of their identity; and communicate their thoughts using complex, meaningful, and mindful language. To accomplish these goals and objectives, students and teachers, in week one, reflect on the pieces that constitute a migrant identity and how these have been dehumanized and stereotyped by oppressing groups (Roer-Strier, Strier, Este, Shimoni, & Clark, 2005; Sassen, 2014). Responding to the question, "who am I?," they compare their experiences with the ones depicted by the aforesaid authors. Following this self-analysis, in week two, students conduct ethnographic and pictographic research by taking pictures of objects, persons, and symbols that define their community. The idea is to contextualize their identity within their communities in order to overcome anonymization and their feelings of lack of belonging. Through digital collages, students present the new identifiers acquired when arriving in a new city or a school. The previous question, *who am I?*, becomes *where do I belong?* The outcome when responding to these questions is, as stated by Howard (2014), to show that high-quality and responsive education is a reality "when we [educators] embrace the richness and complexities that are present in the differences that each of us [educators, migrant students and their families] presents" (p. 8).

In weeks three and four, students and teachers continue deconstructing their identities and rebuilding them by creating "cultural tags" and the culminating project: a Graffiti Wall. Deconstruction in this project is defined, using Newman's (2001) study of Norris's (1987) work on Jacques Derrida's framework, as "a series of moves, which include the dismantling of conceptual oppositions and hierarchical systems of thought"[8] imposed upon migrant students and their families. Students draw their cultural tags to portray their identity and the struggles, successes, and challenges infringed by mobility and hard work, but propelled by commitment to achieve their personal goals. A caption accompanies each cultural tag. The written text in this context is the support rather than the core of the assignment. The words are used, as Freire and Macedo (1987) explain, to read the inner world of migrant students and their families.

All the tags come together to compose a Graffiti Wall, which ensembles the initial, sometimes isolated *I am*, into the intricacy and richness of *the We*. For the past seven years, more than 2,000 migrant students have been assembling Graffiti Walls across California. Students participating in these programs came back to their regular schools empowered and equipped with the tools needed to successfully navigate their educational systems. This empowerment was two-fold: a) the self-esteem, confidence, and knowledge migrant students built, and b) the learning experiences parents and students shared completing the digital collages, and discussing at home the themes inferred from the readings.

76 *Fernando Rodríguez-Valls and Sandra Kofford*

As an interdisciplinary curriculum, Language Explorers supports the language development as well as the critical thinking skills and creativity of PK-12 migrant students. Further, both educators and students have been able to carry the knowledge acquired through the four-week program into their regular school settings.

Data-Driven Decision Programs

A key aspect in these two programs is that they include assessments tools: 1) to evaluate the effectiveness as the programs are being implemented, 2) to measure the expected outcomes, and 3) to modify and adapt future practices. Assessments, as Law and Eckes (2007) explain, are needed because the "federal government demands accountability. . . . Administrators must decide how and into which program to place these students. . . . Teachers need to know how to plan instruction. . . . Parents need to know how children are doing. . . . Students need to know what they have accomplished" (p. 14).

Aligned with this idea, the Family Biliteracy Program and Language Explorers include pre- and post- summative assessments to measure growth in terms of language and content skills and tasks. This growth is key in terms of accountability and programmatic decisions. In addition, both programs have weekly formative assessments designed to assess and monitor students' progress. These assessments inform teaching and learning practices as well as provide the opportunity for students to evaluate their own progress. A third assessment tool is added to these two quantitative measures. Teachers create an individual portfolio displaying all the projects students have completed throughout the program. Projects create the qualitative framework to understand and analyze the quantitative data. Further, students comment on their own portfolios, creating a sense of reflection and self-assessment.

Moreover, some of these projects are utilized to generate the weekly formative assessments. For example, in the Language Explorers program, teachers develop questions on student-generated texts for the assessments. In week one, after students write their poems, teachers select and develop questions on some of these poems. In week two, teachers use some of the pictures and the captions students created for their digital collages. And in week three, teachers pick some cultural tags and the text attached to these to assess students' language skills. In the Family Biliteracy Program, students and parents present their projects in front of the class. Then teachers begin to dialogue with the families on how the skills taught during the week have helped them when completing a family tree, a brochure for a supermarket, or a puppet done with paper plates, yarn, and buttons. Through this dialogue, teachers can informally assess the growth in biliteracy skills for both students and parents.

Incorporating students' work as part of the assessment piece has a two-fold impact on students' performance: a) students' knowledge is validated and b) students' culture and language becomes an intrinsic part of the learning process. Oftentimes, assessment tools, whether standardized or teacher created, tend to reflect an academic language that neither includes students' experiences nor reflects their language and culture. Language Explorers asks teachers to utilize texts created by the students since "language [is] partial, never neutral, and contextually dependent, we [teachers working with migrant students] can ask alternative questions that invite collaborative explorations" with students and their families' funds of knowledge, language, and culture (Van Cleave & Bridges-Rhoads, 2014, p. 42).

All the data generated by these assessments help county offices and school districts when reporting to the Migrant Education Office in the California Department of Education. The data inform administrators and their teams when designing their RAs and DSAs. Ideally teachers would use the information to modify and adapt their practices. Migrant parents whose students are participating in the Family Biliteracy Program and/or Language Explorers are informed about their child's progress, which educates them when providing advice to administrators designing and making programmatic decisions. But, most importantly, all the growth and learning portrayed in these data empower, educate, and equip migrant students with the tools to overcome anonymization and the lack of belonging they may experience in their school sites. Once they are recognized, valued, and have a sense of belonging, the first step towards closing the achievement gap has been accomplished. At this point, educators working with migrant students should realize that, as Sonia Nieto (2013) depicts when quoting an excerpt from the journal *The American Teacher* by Gruenberg (1912): "[migrant] Education must and foremost measure its efficiency . . . in terms to increase humanism, increase power to do, increase capacity to appreciate" (p. 90).

Future Directions

Family Biliteracy and Language Explorers are two examples of programs designed for migrant students and their families. There are a few other programs, such as the Migrant Summer Leadership Institute (MSLI), sponsored by CDE, and the Speech and Debate Program, which have contributed to reinforcing and strengthening college readiness and language and literacy skills, as well as to empowering migrant students. However, there is a need for more programs targeting the specific needs of the migrant population—anonymization and lack of belonging. As Barlett and Garcia (2011) explain, migrant students are exposed to systematic oppression. In terms of income, minimum wages are not always honored by farm owners or the owners of factories or slaughterhouses. They also experience segregation; not only do many migrant families live in migrant camps close to hazardous areas, but their needs are not valued and their linguistic and cultural richness is not included as part of the "mainstream" culture.

Without specific programs for migrant students, politicians and stakeholders could question the need for maintaining migrant funding as an imperative and much needed support. Effective programs such as the ones described in this chapter play a key role in terms of advocacy for migrant education. Moreover, Family Biliteracy and Language Explorers reverse the existing pattern in which migrant students are served with programs designed for other student populations. Family Biliteracy and Language Explorers have already been adapted to be used with EL students. The pattern of migrant education borrowing from other programs has changed to migrant education being the model to be followed by others.

However, the important element is to increase the number of migrant programs that include clear goals and objectives, and which produce optimal outcomes across all the seven areas of Regional Applications (RAs) and District Service Agreements (DSAs). Among these outcomes are: to better prepare migrant students and their families ready to enter kindergarten; to increase the number of migrant students graduating from high school who are ready to attend college or prepare to successfully enter a professional path; to improve nutritional habits; and to educate migrant parents, who can then become activists for better working conditions, advocates for their children's education, and believers that they are an intrinsic part of our society.

If, as Ponlop Ripoche (2010) reminds us, "we can get over our idea that wisdom is exclusive to certain people or groups, then our world expands dramatically" (p. 171). Programs designed to meet and assess the needs of migrant students and their families must be the foundation for a pedagogical switch and educational transformation. Working with migrant students must be seen as a unique learning opportunity for educators to expand their knowledge about their role in education, which is at all times to eliminate suppressing perspectives pushed upon minority groups (Cummins, 2013). This role cannot be fulfilled unless educators prepare themselves to work with, learn from, and embrace the knowledge, languages, and cultures that migrant students and their families cultivate in their households and that society is eager to harvest to improve humanity.

Notes

1 Author 1 is a former Migrant Education Program State Administrator; Author 2 is a current Migrant Education Regional Director.
2 MSIX "is the technology that allows States to share educational and health information on migrant children who travel from State to State and who as a result, have student records in multiple States' information systems" (http://www2. ed.gov/admins/lead/account/recordstransfer.html).
3 34 CFR 200.83: https://www.law.cornell.edu/cfr/text/34/200.83#a_1
4 Program description of the Migrant Education Even Start Program: http://www2. ed.gov/programs/mees/index.html
5 Migrant Education Program SSDP: http://www.cde.ca.gov/sp/me/mt/ssdp.asp
6 Migrant Family Biliteracy Program (MFBP): http://www.cde.ca.gov/sp/me/mt/mef bpbackground.asp

7 Idaho Family Biliteracy: http://www.sde.idaho.gov/el-migrant/migrant/files/migrant-education-plan/_files/SDP/List-of-Service-Strategies.pdf
8 Retrieved on April 15, 2016 from https://theanarchistlibrary.org/library/saul-newman-derrida-s-deconstruction-of-authority

References

Barlett, L. & Garcia, O. (2011). *Additive schooling in subtractive times: Bilingual education and Dominican immigrant youth in the Heights.* Nashville, TN: Vanderbilt University Press.

Cisneros, S. (1991). *The house on Mango Street.* London: Vintage.

Cummins, J. (2013). Language and identity in multilingual schools: Constructing evidence-based instructional policies. In D. Little, C. Leung & P. Van Avermaet (Eds.), *Managing diversity in education: Languages, policies and pedagogies* (pp. 3–26). Ontario, Canada: Multilingual Matters.

Delpit, L. (2006). *Other people's children: Cultural conflict in the classroom.* New York: The New Press.

Echeverría, J., Vogt, M. & Short, D. (2013). *Making content comprehensible for secondary English learners: The SIOP model,* Second Edition. Upper Saddle, NJ: Pearson.

Escamilla, K., Hopewell, S. & Butvilofsky, S. (2013). *Biliteracy from the start: Literacy squared in action.* Philadelphia, PA: Caslon Publishing.

Freire, P. & Macedo, D. (1987). *Reading the word and the world.* Westport, CT: Praeger

García, O. (2009). *Bilingual education in the 21st century: A global perspective.* Malden, MA: Wiley-Blackwell.

García, O. & Kleifgen, J. A. (2010). *Educating emergent bilinguals: Policies, programs and practices for English language learners.* New York: Teachers College Press.

Gay, G. (2010). *Culturally responsive teaching: Theory, research and practice.* New York: Teachers College Press.

Gruenberg, B. C. (1912). Efficiency versus Democracy. *The American Teacher, 1,* 79–81.

Howard, T. C. (2014). *Why race & culture matter in schools: Closing the achievement gap in America's classroom.* New York: Teachers College Press.

Law, B. & Eckes, M. (2007). *Assessment and ESL: An alternative approach.* Winnipeg, Canada: Portage & Main Press.

Lippi-Green, R. (2011). *English with an accent: Language, ideology and discrimination.* New York: Routledge.

Lu, Y. & Zhou, H. (2013). Academic achievement and loneliness of migrant children in China: School segregation and segmented assimilation. *Comparative Education Review, 57*(1), 85–116. http://doi.org/10.1086/667790

Luen Yang, G. (2008). *American born Chinese.* New York: First Second Books.

Luke, A. (2013). The political problem of curriculum making. In A. Luke, A. Woods & K. Weir (Eds.), *Curriculum, syllabus design and equity: A primer model* (pp. 1–6). New York: Routledge.

Martín Peris, E. (2010). ¿A qué nos referimos cuando hablamos de "usar una lengua para aprenderla"? *Bellaterra Journal of Teaching and Learning Language and Literature, 3*(1), 1–18.

80 Fernando Rodríguez-Valls and Sandra Kofford

Moll, L. (2013). *L.S. Vygotsky and education*. New York: Routledge.

Moll, L., Amanti, C., Neff, D. & Gonzalez, N. (1992). Funds of knowledge for teaching: Using a qualitative approach to connect homes and classrooms. *Theory into Practice, 31*(2), 132–141.

NESSE-Education and Migration. (2008). *Strategies for integrating migrant children in European schools and societies: A synthesis of research findings for policy-makers*. Brussels, Belgium: Education & Culture DG.

Newman, S. (2001). Derrida's deconstruction of authority. *Philosophy & Social Criticism, 27*(3). Retrieved from https://theanarchistlibrary.org/library/saul-newman-derrida-s-deconstruction-of-authority

Nieto, S. (2013). *Finding the joy in teaching students of diverse backgrounds: Culturally responsive and socially just practices in U.S. classrooms*. Portsmouth, NH: Heinemann.

Norris, C. (1987). *Derrida*. Boston, MA: Harvard University Press.

Olsen, L. (2010). *Reparable harm: Fulfilling the unkept promise of educational opportunity for California's long term English learners*. Long Beach: California's Together Research & Policy Publication.

Paffey, D. (2014). *Language ideologies and the globalization of "standard" Spanish*. Broadway, NY: Bloomsbury Academic.

Piller, I. (2016). *Linguistic diversity and social justice: An introduction to applied sociolinguistics*. New York: Oxford University Press.

Ponlop, D. (2010). *Rebel Buddha: A guide to a revolution of mind*. Boston, MA: Shambhala Publications.

Prewitt-Diaz, J. O., Trotter, R. T. II. & Rivera, V. A. (1990). *The effects of migration on children: An ethnographic study*. Harrisburg: Pennsylvania Department of Education, Division of Migrant Education.

Quezada, R., Rodríguez-Valls, F. & Lindsey, R. (2016). *Teaching and supporting migrant children in our schools: A culturally proficient approach*. Lanham, MD: Rowman & Littlefield, Inc.

Rodríguez, D., Carrasquillo, A. & Soon Lee, K. (2014). *The bilingual advantage: Promoting academic development, biliteracy, and native language in the classroom*. New York: Teachers College Press.

Rodríguez-Izquierdo, R. M. (2015). Estudio de las actitudes hacia la escuela y de las expectativas educativas de los estudiantes de origen inmigrante. *Education Policy Analysis Archives, 23*(127). Retrieved from http://epaa.asu.edu/ojs/article/view/2161/1707

Rodríguez-Valls, F., Kofford, S. & Morales, E. (2012). Graffiti walls: Migrant students and the art of communicative languages. *Journal of Social Theory in Art Education, 32*, 96–111. Retrieved from http://cstae.org/journal/index.php/jstae/article/view/35/48

Rodríguez-Valls, F., Montoya, M. & Valenzuela, P. (2014). Biliteracy summer schools: Breaking the cycle of monolingualism in migrant families. *Childhood Education, 90*(2), 107–115.

Rodríguez-Valls, F. & Torres, C. (2014). Partnerships and networks in migrant education: Empowering migrant families to support their children's success. *Multicultural Education, 21*(3 & 4), 34–38.

Roer-Strier, D., Strier, R., Este, D., Shimoni, R. & Clark, D. (2005). Fatherhood and immigration: Challenging the deficit theory. *Child and Family Social Work, 10*, 315–329.

Sassen, S. (2014). *Expulsions: Brutality and complexity in the global economy.* Cambridge, MA: Belknap Press.

Shakur, T. (1999). *The rose that grew from concrete.* London: Simon & Schuster.

Shin, S. J. (2012). *Bilingualism in schools and society: Language, identity, and policy.* New York: Routledge.

Soto, G. (2006). *A fire in my hands.* New York: Houghton Mifflin Harcourt.

Thorpe, H. (2011). *Just like us: The true story of four Mexican girls coming of age in America.* New York: Scribner.

Trujillo Sáez, F., Lorenzo, F., y Vez. J. M. (2011). *Educación bilingüe. Integración de contenidos y segundas lenguas.* Madrid, Spain: Editorial Síntesis.

Valdés, G. (2003). *Expanding definitions of giftedness: The case of young interpreters from immigrant communities.* Mahwah, NJ: Lawrence Erlbaum.

Valenzuela, A. (1999). *Subtractive schooling: U.S.-Mexican youth and the politics of caring.* Albany: State University of New York Press.

Valenzuela, A. (2016). *Growing critically conscious teachers: A social justice curriculum for educators of Latino/a youth.* New York: Teachers College Press.Van Cleave, J. & Bridges-Rhoads, S. (2014). Rewriting the common core standards for tomorrow's literacies. *English Journal, 104*(2), 41–47.

Vasquez, V. (2004). *Negotiating critical literacies with young children.* Mahwah, NJ: Lawrence Erlbum.

Žižek, S. (2013). *Demanding the impossible.* Malden, MA: Polity Press.

6 What Can Latina/o Migrant Students Tell Us about College Outreach and Access?

Anne-Marie Núñez

Migrant students are among the most marginalized student populations in the U.S., and have relatively low college-going rates (Velázquez, 1996; Zalaquett, McHatton, & Cranston-Gingras, 2007). A variety of factors in the U.S. political, social, and economic ecology pose challenges to the college access of migrant students. Migrant students are among the poorest students in the U.S. K-12 school system, and tend to be enrolled in the least well-resourced schools in terms of course availability, teacher qualifications, and spending per student (California Department of Education, 2007; Futernick, 2005). Anti-affirmative action, anti-bilingual education, and anti-immigrant policies in effect create an "anti-migrant policy regime" (Núñez & Gildersleeve, 2016, p. 503) that compromises migrant students' academic preparation, the valuation of their academic and leadership potential in the college admissions process, and financial support for college (Núñez & Gildersleeve, 2016; Zavala & Pérez, 2016).

Most college outreach programs emphasize the importance of providing access to academic and financial support, as well as "college knowledge" about the college application and enrollment process (e.g., Perna, Rowan-Kenyon, Bell, Thomas, & Li, 2008; St. John, Hu, & Fisher, 2011). It is critical that college outreach programs serving migrant students focus on these factors. However, as I will argue in this chapter, college outreach for migrant students can be most effective when it also engages migrant students in inquiry regarding the sociopolitical conditions of their communities and of this nation (Jasis & González, this volume).

In this chapter, I will address how migrant students experience multiple (rather than monolithic) social identities and contexts, and experience different kinds of history that condition their college access. Since most migrant students are Latino, I will focus on the relationship between migrant Latino identities. In this case, I will illustrate the importance of using a framework of intersectionality (Núñez, 2014a, 2014b) to conceptualize identities, social contexts, and historical ecologies that are salient to migrant communities. Then, I will show how research based on a successful migrant outreach program demonstrates the importance of taking a holistic approach that weaves together the development of normative and critical skills for

College Outreach and Access   83

college-going and best positions migrant students to address the exclusionary contexts that they navigate. Based on this discussion, I will outline five recommendations to promote migrant students' college access and associated implications.

Contextual and Structural Challenges to Migrant Students' College Access

Although there may be common conceptions of migrant students' backgrounds, migrant students have diverse social identities and inhabit a variety of social contexts (Núñez & Gildersleeve, 2016). For example, some migrant students' families have been in the U.S. for centuries, and others have arrived more recently. Migrant students come from a variety of ethnic backgrounds, including Latino and Asian American. They speak a variety of languages, with differing degrees of proficiency. Migrant students reside in different states with different college access policies.

A multi-level model of intersectionality based on an extensive review of research (Núñez, 2014a, 2014b) provides one way to map the multidimensionality of the contextual and structural elements affecting migrant students' postsecondary opportunities. Figure 6.1 indicates the general model as it applies to the micro-, meso-, and macro-level factors affecting migrant students' college access.

On the first level, this model posits that, in addition to being migrant, these students have multiple social identities that also affect their educational opportunities. Such identities can include race and ethnicity (Latina/o), immigration status, language skills (i.e., the extent to which a student is an English Learner), and citizenship status.

On the second level, the meso-level, migrant students encounter social contexts that can hinder or enhance the extent to which they can maximize their educational potential. These contexts are "domains of power" (Dill & Zambrana, 2009), but also "arenas of practice" (Anthias, 2013; Núñez, 2014a, b) where power dynamics inhibiting migrant students' college access can be disrupted. In the model of intersectionality, these social contexts include organizational, representational, intersubjective, and experiential contexts. As applied to migrant students, *organizational* contexts could include school tracking that tends to place migrant students in fewer college preparatory courses than their counterparts from other backgrounds. The organizational dimension could also include the degree to which the K-12 schools that migrant students attend are well-resourced in terms of the availability of: college preparatory courses, qualified teachers, dedicated counseling oriented towards college, and physical facilities conducive to being able to focus on schoolwork.

Also on the second level, the *representational* dimension includes how migrant students are represented in public, policy, and media discourses. For example, speaking to the relevance of multiple identities, migrant

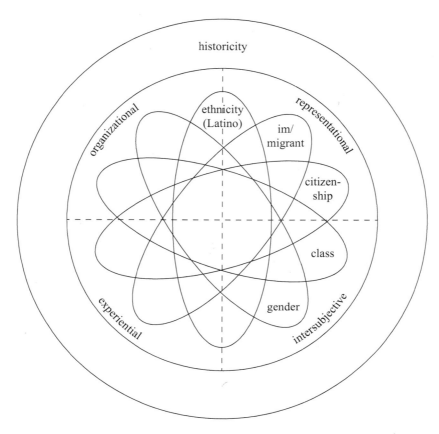

Figure 6.1 Multilevel Model of Intersectionality Among Migrant Student Identities and Contexts. Adapted from Núñez (2014a, 2014b).

identity is often conflated with a Latino identity and an undocumented status identity. Although the majority of Latinos are born in the U.S., one survey indicates that 30% of the public erroneously assumes that the majority of Latinos are "illegal immigrants" (National Hispanic Media Coalition, 2012). Sociologists Massey and Pren (2012) have in fact documented a "Latino threat narrative" in the media that they assert is correlated with increased deportations and hate crimes against Latinos (p. 7). How migrants and Latinos are represented in the media can affect the safety of these groups.

Another aspect of the representational dimension involves how migrant students are represented in educational research and policy discourses. Historically, these students and their families have been framed in deficit terms, with capabilities inferior to those of other communities (Zavala & Pérez, 2016). Alternatively, migrant students and families have been portrayed as victims, powerless to transform their life chances (Zavala & Pérez, 2016). Importantly, these discourses render invisible the agency of migrant students and their communities to create social change, and obscure histories of migrant social movements such as those of the United Farm Workers that mobilized large communities to advocate for social and material recognition of the contributions of the migrant community to the economy.

In a related vein, a third area in the meso-level of factors that migrant students encounter also includes the way that other individuals treat them, or the *intersubjective* dimension. How teachers treat students through the assumptions that they make about students' abilities or the courses that they direct these students to enroll in can have longer-term consequences on students' academic achievement and college preparation (Croninger & Lee, 2001). In their longitudinal study of Latina/o and Asian immigrant students' schooling experiences and academic achievement, Suárez-Orozco and colleagues (2008) found that teachers tended to underrate the abilities of Latina/o immigrant students in relation to those of Asian immigrant students, and that this tendency could have adverse effects on course placement for the Latina/o students. Such inclinations on the part of teachers could reinforce stereotype threat (Steele, 1997, 2010) among immigrant and migrant Latina/o students and perpetuate a cycle of declining academic achievement and college preparation.

Also within the meso-level, the intersectionality model stipulates that a fourth *experiential* dimension affects educational opportunity. The experiential dimension can include internalized narratives and explanations for one's level of academic achievement. For example, the extent to which migrant students may attribute their educational challenges to individual or structural factors can affect their level of academic accomplishment. Migrant students who internalize dominant narratives that their abilities are inferior (an aspect of stereotype threat) may lose confidence about their abilities, and this can have adverse consequences for their school engagement and achievement (Gibson & Hildalgo, 2009). However, migrant students who are invited to engage in the sociopolitical realities and histories that have limited the life chances of migrant families, including poor schooling and negative stereotypes about migrant students' abilities, can come to see that societal institutions may in fact carry much of the responsibility for their limited access to postsecondary opportunities (Gildersleeve, 2010; Núñez & Gildersleeve, 2016; Pacheco & Nao, 2009).

Finally, the third level of the model of intersectionality stipulates that historicity—the historical context that shapes various arenas of power at a given moment in time—will by extension shape educational opportunities for migrant students. Migrant students and families have faced a long history in which dominant institutions, including education, housing, and labor, have excluded them from full civil and human rights (Zavala & Pérez, 2016). Currently, migrant students encounter a broader policy climate that presents at least three strands that compromise college access:

anti-immigrant, anti-bilingual education, and anti-affirmative action policies (Núñez & Gildersleeve, 2016). The current nativism in the U.S. is particularly directed at Latinos; one survey indicated that most Latinos anticipate that, regardless of their immigration status, they expect to be apprehended by law enforcement (e.g., stopped by the police to have their identification checked) in some way in the future (Menjívar & Abrego, 2012). K-12 bilingual education programs have been banned in certain states, although intentional immersion in dual languages has been shown to be positively associated with academic achievement (Gándara & Hopkins, 2010; Gándara & Orfield, 2010). Unfortunately, then, these education programs have been banned in certain places on the basis of political ideology, rather than what works best for these students. Anti-affirmative action policies have been associated with declines in application rates and consequent enrollment among Latinas/os and African Americans at selective public universities (Brown & Hirschman, 2006; Oakes et al., 2006), which are often the most affordable selective institutions that historically underserved students like migrants can afford.

Together, the marginalized status of several social identities that are often related to a "migrant" identity and oppressive power dynamics in various social contexts that blame migrant students for structural constraints that hinder their advancement and nativist trends all pose challenges for migrant students seeking to pursue higher education. How, then, can practitioners and policymakers broaden opportunities within the current societal climate affecting migrant students? How can researchers frame their inquiry in ways that emphasize migrant students' agency to pursue higher education within the face of political, economic, and social challenges? Research based on the experiences and outcomes of a migrant outreach program that increased college access indicates that centering migrant students' perspectives reveals important strategies that can expand their college access (Núñez, 2014a; Núñez & Gildersleeve, 2016). Now, I will address this research and its implications for broadening migrant students' college access.

Student Perspectives from the Migrant Student Leadership Institute

Here, I review critical research on migrant student college access regarding research on the Migrant Student Leadership Institute (MSLI), an annual summer five-week program serving migrant students around the state of California about to enter their senior year in high school who have been selected from their respective high schools for academic and leadership abilities. Initially designed by scholar Kris Gutiérrez at UCLA, the goals and intentions of program activities are two-fold: (1) to prepare students to become leaders of their communities, and (2) to promote college enrollment in selective public higher education (particularly University of California campuses). While earning at least a 3.0 GPA is a prerequisite to entering the program, student participants are also selected based on relatively low scores on standardized tests in reading and writing (Núñez & Gildersleeve, 2016). Most program participants attend California high schools that send relatively few Latino or underrepresented students to four-year public institutions in California. Consistent with broader representation of Latinos among migrant students and families, almost all participants (97%) are Latino.

Importantly, the program is organized to cultivate sociocritical literacy around college-going, in addition to enhancing students' academic skills and knowledge about the college application process. Sociocritical literacy is conceptualized as "a syncretic literacy organized around a pedagogical approach that focuses on how individuals and their *communities* influence and are influenced by *social, political, and cultural discourses and practices* in historically specific times and locations" (Gutiérrez, 2008, p. 150, emphasis added). Importantly then, the program not only focuses on encouraging students to develop individual agency regarding their postsecondary trajectories, but to situate that agency within historically asymmetrical political, economic, and social power dynamics that have constrained migrant students' college access as well as limited migrant families' opportunities to pursue economic stability, well-being, and participation in a democratic society.

Program activities focus on developing: (1) students' academic literacy, primarily through writing in different genres, (2) college-going literacy, through learning about applying for college and financial aid, and (3) sociocritical literacy. Activities include encouraging students to communicate in any languages (e.g., English and Spanish) in which they feel comfortable, addressing scientific academic content through exploration of social issues (like public health) with Latino role models, and interrogating sociopolitical conditions that historically have limited migrant students' and families' life chances.

Multiple research methods have been used to study MSLI participants' college outreach and access experiences and outcomes. Together, these analyses indicate that the program appears to expand college access for these students (Núñez & Gildersleeve, 2016). Namely, quantitative longitudinal studies of students' application and enrollment outcomes suggest that, compared with a group of similarly skilled migrant students who did not participate in the program, MSLI program participants are far more likely to apply and enroll in the most selective public higher education sector in California (the University of California system) (Núñez, 2009). This finding begs the question: what influence does the cultivation of academic, college-going, and/or sociocritical literacy have on college access for these migrant students? More specifically, since research has documented the importance of normative, traditional outreach activities (e.g., St. John, Hu, & Fisher, 2011)—that is, developing academic skills, financial knowledge, and college knowledge in promoting college access, does the program's additional emphasis on the development of sociocritical literacy

88 *Anne-Marie Núñez*

also account for the increase in college access for these students (Núñez & Gildersleeve, 2016)?

In qualitative investigations of the program, students express that in fact, the program activities emphasizing sociocritical literacy have uniquely contributed to expanding their sense of postsecondary possibilities (Gildersleeve, 2010; Núñez & Gildersleeve, 2016). Specifically, they express how the program helped them with four critical dimensions that promote access to college: sharpening writing skills, college planning, visiting a college campus, and financing college. While these dimensions have been identified in other research on more traditional outreach programs (e.g., Perna et al., 2008; St. John et al., 2011), the students' descriptions of the benefits of these activities go beyond traditional frameworks of college access and outreach that solely emphasize academic and college-going literacy.

Specifically, with regard to sharpening writing skills, students not only talked about increasing their academic ability, but increasing their sense of ownership and voice through having their linguistic backgrounds be positioned in the program as something to be built on, rather than denigrated. One student talked about how before the program, school personnel assumed he could not write, because his family did not speak English. After engaging in MSLI's activities of writing, the student presented his essay to his teachers, who recognized that the student was far more talented than they had assumed.

With regard to college planning, students discussed developing a sense of entitlement to pursuing selective public higher education, though they saw few individuals from their backgrounds as students or faculty on the UCLA campus. They realized that campuses like UCLA were supposed to serve them, even if historically these campuses had not enrolled many of them. This recognition complemented quantitative findings that migrant program participants, compared with equivalent non-participants, were far more likely to apply to and be admitted to UC campuses.

Building on the point above, although students saw few individuals from their backgrounds in the UCLA campus, students described how they challenged the image of campus through recognizing and connecting with the dining staff, groundskeepers, and custodians, who were more likely than students or faculty to be from Latino backgrounds. As one student put it:

> Our classes were teaching us about economics and equitable labor practices and all. Then we'd go eat dinner, and we're the only ones treating kitchen staff like we treat our parents. It was deeper than language. It was like recognizing those labor inequities like pay and hours and benefits right in our faces.

Thus the process of visiting a college campus while recognizing sociocritical considerations helped the students feel a greater sense of belonging, possibility, and entitlement in going to UCLA, while also being critical of the exclusionary conditions of the system of higher education.

In terms of financing college, students described how workshops targeting unique challenges they could encounter in completing a FAFSA prepared them better to take this critical step in accessing resources for college. One student discussed how a class conversation about the DREAM Act informed him about college possibilities and sparked his thinking about how to pay for college. Another discussed learning a more nuanced way to approach college applications by separating admissions and the financial aid process and realizing unique ways to report their family's income through seasonal earnings, a category that is not obvious or explicit in the FAFSA.

Put differently, to apply Núñez's (2014a, 2014b) model of intersectionality, the program recognizes the multiple identities of migrant students and creates space for migrant students to affirm and incorporate such identities—including language, national origin, and citizenship—into their planning for college. With respect to the four social contexts as described in the model, the program supports students in addressing the organizational dimension of their schooling by enhancing their academic skills and building on (rather than ignoring or denigrating) the literacies they brought to the classroom. In the representational context, the program helps students to challenge negative representations of migrant students and families. With respect to the intersubjective context, the students described developing meaningful and trusting relationships with their instructors, which encouraged them to build confidence in and forge their own voices in writing without fear of being judged or criticized on the basis of superficial assumptions about their abilities. In terms of the experiential dimension of the model, students described expanding their perceptions about opportunities for higher education and their own "merit," deservingness, and entitlement to pursue higher education, especially selective higher education in an anti-affirmative action state policy context such as California.

More broadly, speaking to the intersectionality level of historicity (Núñez, 2014a, 2014b), students express that learning more about historical, social, and political forces that affected the life chances of migrant families helped them realize that migrant families' limited opportunities were due to exclusionary factors in the structural fabric of U.S. society. Through activities challenging anti-bilingual education, anti-immigrant, and anti-affirmative policy forces, students' sense of possibilities for their higher education prospects expanded. In sum, attending to these students' perspectives teaches us that in outreach and in promoting college access, it is important to engage their sociopolitical realities as well as cultivate their academic skills and college knowledge.

Recommendations

In this chapter, I have centered migrant students' perspectives in broadening the understanding of how to enhance migrant postsecondary opportunity through efforts such as college outreach. Now, I propose recommendations that recognize how the sociopolitical realities that migrant students

90   *Anne-Marie Núñez*

encounter are closely intertwined with the academic, financial, and cultural challenges they face in college access. The strategies suggested below are intended to inform outreach program developers or institutional agents like teachers and counselors about how to support migrant students in navigating the current policy ecology concerning college access.

First, Cultivate Ownership of and Engagement in the Development of Academic Skills, Particularly Writing

Migrant students may lack confidence in their writing skills due to issues such as poor instruction, marginalization in schools, or limited exposure to teaching that builds on the language skills they bring to the classroom. Offering migrant students opportunities to write in different academic genres and the freedom to express themselves in multiple languages, if they would like (Rodríguez-Valls and Kofford, this volume), helps migrant students see the relevance of academic literacy as distinct from other kinds of language literacy (Scarcella, 2003). If these students can strengthen their writing, they can strengthen their ownership of their academic expression and voice, while retaining other community-oriented forms of expression. This ownership can support the development of other academic skills such as reading, math, and scientific reasoning.

Second, Provide Migrant Students with Tools to Plan for Their College Educations

This process includes involving students in drafting their own plans for applying to and choosing from various postsecondary options. It involves exposing these students to on-campus experiences in different kinds of postsecondary institutions of varying degrees of selectivity and cost, and including public and private institutions, as well as community colleges. Visiting college campuses helps students envision themselves more clearly on these campuses.

Third, as Part of Providing Migrant Students with Tools to Plan for Their College Educations, Offer Students Extensive and Hands-on Guidance in Completing Federal Financial Aid Forms

Research has shown that questions asked in financial aid forms may not align with the realities of historically underserved groups and those from low-income backgrounds (Bloom, 2007). Targeted support about how to address questions about family income (when that income might be seasonal and not annual, for example), would help these students depict their families' realities more specifically (Bettinger, Long, Oreopoulos, & Sanbonmatus, 2009; Núñez & Gildersleeve, 2016). Engaging migrant students in connecting their lived realities with the complexities of financial aid forms can be particularly beneficial for migrant students who are undocumented (Núñez & Gildersleeve, 2016; Zarate, 2006).

Fourth, Engage Students in Interrogating Deficit Views of Their Own Abilities That They May Be Receiving from Teachers, Administrators, the Media, Their Families, or the Broader Policy Ecology

This process involves exercises to identify these deficit views and challenging these views with a better understanding of migrant students' historical, social, and economic conditions that reveal conceptions of entities like merit as being socially constructed. More broadly, this process can encourage students to remain connected with their communities of origin as they pursue postsecondary education. Maintaining such ties is important for more seamless college transitions (e.g., Hurtado & Carter, 1997; Núñez, 2005).

Fifth, Weave Efforts to Engage the Lived Sociopolitical Realities of Migrant Students into All Dimensions of College Outreach Efforts

Clearly, migrant students are well aware of the power dynamics in society limiting their educational opportunities. Educating students about the structural dynamics that limit the advancement of people from marginalized groups, particularly inequities in school finance, access to qualified teachers, treatment of students from different backgrounds, and tracking, helps students to enact their capabilities within a broader context and involves students in challenging dominant narratives such as the myth that all educational advancement is based purely on a singular definition of merit. Through such activities, students build individual agency to recast their future trajectories within an educational system that historically has not been conducive to their success.

Implications

Framings of migrant students and their families in "deficit" or "victim" terms (Zavala & Pérez, 2016) can result in the development of outreach programs that are compensatory—seeking to make up for migrant students' perceived deficiencies. However, the Migrant Student Leadership Institute provides a corrective to this tendency by providing migrant students opportunities to affirm their cultural and community assets and to, more broadly, develop their own agency to pursue higher education. Centering migrant students' perspectives disrupts dominant traditions of building college outreach programs that focus primarily on compensating for migrant students' perceived weaknesses and building academic, financial, and cultural resources that are typically defined by and valued in the dominant culture. These perspectives can inform the development of more holistic outreach programs that encourage students from non-dominant communities not only to learn the

92 *Anne-Marie Núñez*

skills necessary to prepare for, apply for, and enroll in college, but to critically interrogate and challenge existing sociopolitical realities and broader dynamics of economic, social, and political exclusion.

References

Anthias, F. (2013). Intersectional what? Social divisions, intersectionality, and levels of analysis. *Ethnicities, 13*(1), 3–19.

Bettinger, E. P., Long, B. T., Oreopoulos, P. & Sanbonmatus, L. (2009). *The role of simplification and information in college decisions: Results from the H&R Block FAFSA experiment.* Cambridge, MA: National Bureau of Economic Research Working Paper 15361.

Bloom, J. (2007). (Mis)reading social class in the journey towards college: Youth development in America. *Teachers College Record, 109*(2), 343–368.

Brown, S. K. & Hirschman, C. (2006). The end of affirmative action in Washington State and its impact on the transition from high school to college. *Sociology of Education, 79*(2), 106–130.

California Department of Education. (2007). *California migrant program: Comprehensive needs assessment.* Sacramento: Author.

Croninger, R. C. & Lee, V. E. (2001). Social capital and dropping out of high school: Benefits to at-risk students of teachers' support and guidance. *Teachers College Record, 103*(4), 548–581.

Dill, B. T. & Zambrana, R. E. (2009). Critical thinking about inequality: An emerging lens. In B. T. Dill & R. E. Zambrana (Eds.), *Emerging intersections: Race, class, and gender in theory, policy, and practice* (pp. 1–21). New Brunswick, NJ: Rutgers University Press.

Futernick, K. (2005). *Teacher qualification index web page* [Data file]. Retrieved from Education for Democracy web page, http://www.edfordemocracy.org

Gándara, P. & Hopkins, M. (Eds.) (2010). *Forbidden language: English learners and restrictive language policies.* New York: Teachers College Press.

Gándara, P. & Orfield, G. (2010). Moving from failure to a new vision of language policy. In P. Gándara & M. Hopkins (Eds.), *Forbidden language: English learners and restrictive language policies* (pp. 216–226). New York: Teachers College Press.

Gibson, M. A. & Hidalgo, N. D. (2009). Bridges to success in high school for migrant youth. *Teachers College Record, 111*(3), 683–711.

Gildersleeve, R. (2010). *Fracturing opportunity: Mexican migrant students and college-going literacy.* New York: Peter Lang.

Gutiérrez, K. (2008). Developing a sociocritical literacy in the third space. *Reading Research Quarterly, 43*(2), 148–164.

Hurtado, S. & Carter, D. F. (1997). Effects of college transition and perceptions of the campus racial climate on Latino college students' sense of belonging. *Sociology of Education, 70*(1), 342–345.

Massey, D. S. & Pren, K. A. (2012). Origins of the new Latino underclass. *Race and Social Problems, 4*, 5–17.

Menjívar, C. & Abrego, L. (2012). *Legal violence in the lives of immigrants: How immigration enforcement affects families, schools, and workplaces.* Washington, DC: Center for American Progress.

College Outreach and Access 93

National Hispanic Media Coalition. (2012). *The impact of media stereotypes on opinions and attitudes toward Latinos.* Retrieved from http://www.nhmc.org/sites/default/files/LD%20NHMC%20Poll%20Results%20Sept.2012.pdf

Núñez, A.-M. (2005). Negotiating ties: A qualitative study of first-generation female students' transitions to college. *Journal of the First-Year Experience and Students in Transition, 17*(2), 87–118.

Núñez, A.-M. (2009). Creating pathways to college for migrant students: Assessing a migrant outreach program. *Journal of Education for Students Placed at Risk (JESPAR), 14*(3), 226–237.

Núñez, A.-M. (2014a). Advancing an intersectionality framework in higher education: Power and Latino postsecondary opportunity. *Handbook of Theory and Research in Higher Education, 29*, 33–92.

Núñez, A.-M. (2014b). Employing multilevel intersectionality in educational research: Latino identities, contexts, and college access. *Educational Researcher, 43*(2), 85–92.

Núñez, A.-M. & Gildersleeve, R. (2016). Sociocritical matters: Migrant students' college access. *Educational Policy, 30*, 501–535.

Oakes, J., Rogers, J., Silver, D., Valladares, S., Terriquez, V., McDonough, P., Renee, M. & Lipton, M. (2006). *Removing the roadblocks: Fair college opportunities for all California students.* Los Angeles: UC All Campus Consortium for Research on Diversity and UCLA Institute for Democracy, Education, and Access.

Pacheco, M. & Nao, K. (2009). Rewriting identities: Using historicized writing to promote migrant students' writing. *Pedagogies, 4*(1), 24–43.

Perna, L. W., Rowan-Kenyon, H., Bell, A., Thomas, S. L. & Li, C. (2008). A typology of federal and state programs designed to promote college enrollment. *The Journal of Higher Education, 79*(3), 243–267.

Scarcella, R. (2003). *Academic English: A conceptual framework.* Irvine: University of California Linguistic Minority Research Institute.

Steele, C. (1997). A threat in the air. *American Psychologist, 52*(6), 613–629.

Steele, C. (2010). *Whistling Vivaldi.* New York: W. W. Norton and Company.

St. John, E., Hu, S. & Fisher, A. S. (2011). *Breaking through the access barrier: How academic capital formation can improve policy in higher education.* New York: Routledge.

Suárez-Orozco, C., Suárez-Orozco, M. & Todorova, I. (2008). *Learning a new land: Im/migrant students in American society.* Cambridge, MA: Belknap.

Velázquez, L. (1996). Voices from the fields: Community-based migrant education. *New Directions for Adult and Continuing Education, 70*, 27–35.

Zalaquett, C. P., McHatton, P. A. & Cranston-Gingras, A. (2007). Characteristics of Latina/o migrant farmworker students attending a large Metropolitan University. *Journal of Hispanic Higher Education, 6*(2), 135–156.

Zarate, M. E. (2006). *Perceptions of financial aid among California Latino youth. Policy Brief.* Los Angeles: Tomas Rivera Policy Institute.

Zavala, M. & Pérez, P. A. (2016). *A critical historical analysis of migrant education policy texts.* Washington, DC: Annual Meeting of the American Research Association.

7 Migrant Education and Shifting Consciousness

A Cultural Wealth Approach to Navigating Politics, Access, and Equity

Cristina Alfaro, Karen Cadiero-Kaplan, and Sera Hernandez

> Mobility is not just another variable in the life of the migrant child, it is the child's life. It defines the child's world and his/her relationship with the world. Children may live for short periods of time during each year in several communities, sometimes in two, four, six, or even eight different states. Even though their families may have well-established migratory routes, there is no assurance that while on the trek, they will reside in the same communities year after year.
>
> (Green, 2003, p. 62)

Green's (2003) quote above illustrates the socio-cultural reality of the many migrant children and youth attending U.S. schools. This reality is part and parcel of conditions of extreme marginalization (Lopez, 2001, 2004; Zalaquett, Alvarez McHatton, & Cranston-Gingras, 2007), and includes severe economic disadvantages (Kandel, 2008), food insecurities (Borre, Ertle, & Graff, 2010), work-related health conditions, inadequate housing, and occupational hazards (Farmworker Justice, 2013).

It has been well documented that migrant students face multiple barriers to academic achievement, including: the lack of educational continuity in their schooling experiences (Solis, 2004), the inability to enroll and participate in rigorous, college preparatory coursework, and the lack of access to fully qualified or adequately prepared teachers and staff as well as to additional instructional resources and information related to higher education or postsecondary vocational options (Suárez-Orozco, Suárez-Orozco, & Sattin-Bajaj, 2010). Further, students who are English learners lack the opportunity to participate in the same rigorous and challenging grade-level content coursework as their peers due in part to their interrupted schooling and inconsistent instruction in English (Branz-Spall, Rosenthal, & Wright, 2003; Kindler, 2002; LaCroix, 2007; Salinas & Fránquiz, 2004). As a result, these barriers to academic achievement jeopardize migrant students' ability to graduate from high school and continue with postsecondary education (Lundy-Ponce, 2010).

In spite of these challenges, migrant children bring many benefits to the classroom, including "optimism, high aspirations, dedicated hard work, positive attitudes toward school, and the ethic of family support for learning [which] contribute to the fact that some immigrant youth in some countries educationally outperform their native-born peers of comparable backgrounds" (Suárez-Orozco, Suárez-Orozco, C., & Sattin-Bajaj, 2010, p. 38). Recognizing the tension between educational advantages and barriers that migrant students face, the authors examine the role Migrant Education programs in California play in supporting this unique population of students in public schools. As educators living and working in California, the authors engaged in policy and field research and entered into this work from varying perspectives to examine how success for students is defined and measured. Success, in this context, is considered from federal and state level policy directives and direct field experience with migrant youth. Thus, the authors draw from their own work within California Migrant Education from macro- to micro- levels, where their experiences and student data serve as the point of examination of how policy from the federal and state levels is enacted and carried out in the local context.

With this in mind, the authors consider their positionality (Rosaldo, 1989) as a critical aspect of the research process. The first author of this chapter has a migrant family background, is a graduate of Mini-Corps,[1] and is currently working with migrant youth and communities in Southern California. The second author served as the State Migrant Director at the California Department of Education for three years, where one of her major responsibilities was to implement accountability measures to ensure that funding was supportive of student services. At the same time, she also had the responsibility of responding to the Office of Migrant Education (OME) to document inconsistencies in the state's data reporting. The third author has experience working with local Migrant Education programs in San Joaquin County in California as a language and literacy consultant.

Herein, the authors write from the position of scholars working with migrant youth and communities along the Mexico-California border, a demarcation too often perceived as a way of dividing or separating individuals, families, communities, cultures, and languages. Typically borders refer to political boundaries that national governments have created to separate one country from another, such as the border between Mexico and Southern California. However, such political and individual divisions are not that easily demarcated, since in these border communities individuals find themselves living fluidly in between the languages, cultures, and politics of two nations (Relano Pastor, 2007).

Given this reality, the largest group of migrant families move between California and Mexico, and "most migrant workers in California are Latino, primarily from Mexico" (CDE, 2012, p. ii); thus, the ethnographic data shared is directly related to the local border context from where students' and two high school teachers' voices were gathered. These students

96 *Cristina Alfaro et al.*

who live and work on both sides of the border, and two of their teachers, provide narratives which are juxtaposed with state level policy and goals.

Utilizing Ricento and Hornberger's (1996) "onion metaphor," this chapter begins by unpacking how policy informs definitions of success and its intersections with stakeholders from varying levels. The metaphor of the "onion" is a multilayered and ethnographic approach to language policy and planning. This framework allows for and validates spaces of agency where "local actors implement, interpret, and perhaps resist policy initiatives in varying and unique ways" (Hornberger & Johnson, 2007, p. 509). In our conceptualization, the outer layer of policy consists of key mandates put forth by the federal Office of Migrant Education (OME) and enacted by the Migrant Education Program (MEP) via the California Department of Education (CDE). The second layer reflects the evaluation and examination of this policy, and the inner most layer (core/heart) represents the voices of youth.

We contextualize the students' narratives and juxtapose them with federal and state measures for academic success employing Yosso's (2005) framework of cultural wealth. This framework allows for a movement of analysis away from "deficit view of communities of color as places full of cultural poverty disadvantages, and instead focus on the array of cultural knowledge, skills, abilities and contacts possessed by socially marginalized groups that often go unrecognized and unacknowledged" (p. 1). As a result, the framework contextualizes the challenges towards academic success through the voices of migrant youth, and their lived realities and experiences inform the conditions that foster resiliency to overcome barriers to achievement and academic success. The students' voices were documented as *testimonios*, a research tool utilized to obtain the stories shared by migrant youth. *Testimonios* are powerful safe spaces where participants share their voices, reducing the researcher subjectivity often related with qualitative research (Bustos Flores, 2016). While *testimonios* are not commonly referred to in qualitative methodologies, they are a more personal and authentic form of oral narratives and have relevancy for Latino scholars working in majority Latino/border communities. In this chapter, four migrant student *testimonios* were culled for evidence of support systems that assisted youths' abilities to stay in school and in some cases become academically successful. An additional *testimonio* was elicited from one high school teacher working with these migrant youth.

This contextual framing highlights the tension between the macro- lens (or outer layer of the onion) and inner layer of policy enactment (Ricento & Hornberger, 1996). The outer layer is the naming and framing of the policy, while the inner layer is how the policy is enacted, evaluated, and researched from varying ideological perspectives and metrics. This second layer includes academic metrics, or the determination of what counts as student success. This then leads us to the third layer, the core or "heart" of Ricento and Hornberger's (1996) framework, which is the classroom space, or in the case of migrant education, the lived educational spaces that are both inside and outside formal classroom spaces. As Hornberger and Johnson (2007) explain:

> An ethnography of language policy can include textual and historical analysis of policy texts but must be based on ethnographic understandings of some local context. The texts are not without the human agents who act as interpretive conduits between language and policy levels (or layers of LPP and the onion).
>
> (p. 528)

Migrant education policy, even if not specific to language, includes varying language and textual elements that cannot be examined without clear connections to human agency and programmatic expectations. The chapter concludes by juxtaposing the state level criteria and expectations with the lived reality at the local level, where each layer exposes a different purpose or value for success but shares the ultimate goal of educational equity and success for migrant children and youth.

The Outer Layer: Federal and State Education Policy

To address the needs of this population in school settings, the U.S. Department of Education provides states with funding. As part of this most recent reauthorization, ESSA, the federal funding formula is designed to ensure that funds are reaching the states with the highest migrant student populations, including California, with 112,000 migrant students. ESSA indicates that services be prioritized for preschool-aged migrant children and migrant students who have dropped out of school (U.S. Department of Education, 2015). The sections that follow outline state responsibilities to the federal government entitlement programs. This brief overview provides the context in which the MEP is enacted at the state level and identifies both opportunities and challenges as MEP relates to Title I and Title III programs.

Intersecting Educational Entitlement Programs

To provide an understanding of the layers of policy and complexity of engagement from the state to the local level, we place Title I Part C for Migrant Education in the context of Title I Part A: *Improving the Academic Achievement of the Disadvantaged* and Title III: *English Language Acquisition, Language Enhancement, and Academic Achievement Act* entitlement programs. For example, Title I Local Educational Agencies (LEAs) receive federal funds via the State Educational Agency (SEA). In California, the California Department of Education (CDE) distributes these funds to school sites directly. "Title I funded schools are either targeted assistance schools or school wide program schools" where funds are "used to support

98   Cristina Alfaro et al.

effective, research-based educational strategies that close the achievement gap between high-and low-performing students and enable the students to meet the state's challenging academic standards" (CDE, Title I, 2016b). The actual formula is more complex than described here; however, in its basic concept the funds are determined based on student enrollment and socio-economic status. For Title I, funds flow from the SEA to the LEA site to provide academic services and supports for students who are in this categorical program. As a result, this funding source captures those migrant students who are in the low socioeconomic category. The academic link for Title I is the collection of data on academic achievement in Reading/Language Arts and Math that is measured by state level testing, such as the California Standards Tests,[2] where LEAs submit annual assessment data to the state data system for reporting.

Title III is designated specifically for services for students identified as English Language Learners (EL) or immigrants, and is distributed to LEAs from the SEA as with Title I. In this instance, the funding is based on the number of students who are identified by state criteria as EL or immigrant (CDE, Title III, 2016c). Title III funding is also formula based, goes to the LEA, and is used to provide supplemental services for EL students that are beyond what is required by state mandate (e.g., curriculum for ELs) and above Title I (e.g., programs to meet students' needs due to poverty). Therefore, a migrant student would most likely be attending a school that receives Title I programs in addition to free and reduced lunch. Additionally, if that student is identified as an English Learner, then the student could also be benefitting from supplemental EL programs supported by Title III funds. This leaves the migrant funds to be used for services unique to migrant students and go beyond the services being provided by Title I and Title III.

Policy for Migrant Education in the State of California

> The Migrant Education Program in California has provided a wealth of services to migrant students since 1968, including home and center-based preschool programs, emergency medical and dental services, referrals to health care providers, tutoring and extended instructional time, comprehensive summer school, and support for out of school youth. Services such as these have been essential in preparing and supporting migrant students to be successful in school. Nevertheless, a significant achievement gap persists between migrant and non-migrant students.
>
> (CDE, 2012, p. ii)

According to the CDE Migrant Education Program website, California administers the largest migrant program in the country, with funding of approximately $128.6 million that is distributed to the California Department of Education (CDE), which then provides funds to 21 Regional Offices and their respective LEAs. The funds are used to provide services to the approximately 112,000 migrant students in 565 school districts throughout

California, which makes up over half of all the school districts in the state (U.S. Department of Education, 2016a). This amount is provided annually via a fiscal formula based on the state's per pupil expenditure for education and counts of eligible migratory children, age three through 21, residing in California until they attain a high school diploma or the equivalent (U.S. Department of Education, 2016b).

Migrant eligibility is established by federal law and enacted in California, where migrant education services are a priority for those students whose education has been interrupted during the current school year and who are failing, or who are most at risk of failing, to meet state content and performance standards (Legislative Analyst's Office Report, 2006). Unlike federal programs like Title I, Part A or Title III, where students are identified by the LEA via school enrollment or academic measures, migrant students are identified by a qualified migrant recruiter. The recruiter is an individual hired by the MEP regional office who interviews and visits both home and employment locations for migrant workers to determine eligibility for services (Salinas and Franquiz, 2004). These data are then reported to the LEA and SEA. This process is unlike any other educational program in terms of how funding is distributed based on the identification of family status as a migrant worker, rather than socioeconomic status. This added complexity for determining services and related funding is made by a personal connection; one that is made often times outside of a school setting. The settings in which students are identified can be in the parent's place of employment, the family home, or in a community space. Further, unlike Title I or Title III, a young adult may also qualify if they, and not their parents, have moved under the same criteria noted above. These students are identified as Out-of-School-Youth (OSY), who can range in age from 13 to 22. According to research conducted by Hill and Hayes (2007), more than half of the 265,000 identified as OSY live away from their parents. The report found several key differences between out-of-school and in-school youth, notably that "62 percent of out-of-school immigrant youth report an inability to speak English 'well' or 'very well,' but the same is true for only 15 percent of those in school" (p. 1). These data illustrate yet another lived reality that is not always recognized in reporting data for achievement and services, since these students are not only mobile, but work as laborers while attempting to achieve a public education.

Migrant Education Accountability

At the state level, one of the main tasks in administering the Migrant Education Program is to ensure that funding supports appropriate supplemental programs and that those programs are administered in a manner that is fiscally responsible and demonstrates academic achievement. The second author, as an educator and researcher who had been accustomed to the university and K-12 setting, led one of the largest Migrant Education

100   *Cristina Alfaro et al.*

programs in the country; therefore being responsible for programming as a state-level administrator was a new experience. At the CDE, the main drivers were funding and policy regulations, which in turn served as key metrics for determining success. This challenge can be illustrated via one example by contrasting the Federal Government Performance and Results Act (GPRA), which required states receiving migrant funds to report specific data on student achievement with state criteria for supplementary services outlined in the 2010 Comprehensive Needs Assessment (CNA) for California.

The GPRAs were developed collaboratively at the federal level by state leaders in Migrant Education and include four annual measures that each state is required to utilize to create a performance plan and to report annually to the Office of Migrant Education (OME). The four measures are:

1   The percentage of MEP students that scored at or above proficient on their state's annual Reading/Language Arts assessments in grades 3 through 8;
2   The percentage of MEP students that scored at or above proficient on their state's annual Mathematics assessments in grades 3 through 8;
3   The percentage of MEP students who were enrolled in grades 7 through 12, and graduated or were promoted to the next grade level, and;
4   The percentage of MEP students who entered 11th grade that had received full credit for Algebra I (U.S. Department of Education, 2016b).

It is important to note all states are required to report data on services provided and number of students enrolled in programs; however, academic data are considered the metric for success. Additionally, in order for data to be accurately reported to the federal government, the local education agencies (LEAs) administering the program are responsible for reporting the achievement data in Reading/Language Arts, Math, and graduation rates to the state annually. In contrast, the CNA, a required periodic needs assessment document submitted to OME, is extensive in scope and content as it addresses all aspects of Migrant Education programs, and as a result goes far beyond the annual GPRA metrics to include data on all migrant services. Together these data are incorporated into the State Service Delivery Plan (SSDP). The SSDP makes clear that MEP funds are to be utilized for supplementary services for migratory children to ensure that migratory children/ youth:

- who move among the states are not penalized in any manner by disparities among states in curriculum, graduation requirements, or state academic content and student academic achievement standards;
- are provided with appropriate educational services (academic and support) that address their special needs;

- receive full and appropriate opportunities to meet the same challenging state academic content and achievement standards that all children are expected to meet;
- have opportunities and services to overcome educational disruption, cultural and language barriers, social isolation, various health-related problems, and other factors that inhibit the ability of such children to make a successful transition to postsecondary education or employment; and
- benefit from state and local systemic reforms (CDE, 2016a, MEP Overview).

Thus, the SSDP ensures that the challenges of a migratory life are addressed and that funds and program services are aligned to ensure this success. Nonetheless, the language utilized within the administration of the program, from the federal and state levels, emphasizes review and compliance with academic measures. To this end, the overall work of the SEA becomes one of reviewing regional plans which include complex budgets that require specific dollar amounts matched to specific supplemental services. For example, a program may allocate $15,000 towards a summer program curriculum. To be approved, this proposed expenditure would not only have to be supplemental to Title I and Title III, but it would also have to demonstrate that the curriculum can improve academic achievement or GPRA measures. The ultimate responsibility of the state agency is to monitor state regional offices. The responsibility of the LEAs is to ensure funds are being used appropriately and that programs are showing student growth in areas of Reading/Language Arts, Math, and increasing graduation rates, which are determined by either local measures or state summative assessments. However, given the mobility of the population, these data are inconsistent at best, since many migrant students may miss the annual testing window or take the tests when they have only been at the particular school site for three months. As Green (2003) points out, "Children may live for short periods of time during each year in several communities, sometimes in two, four, six, or even eight different states" (p. 62).

Such metrics and processes measuring funding aligned with program outcomes represent the outer layer of the "onion" metaphor, where policy is developed by stakeholders with intentions to measure success and hold schools accountable for student achievement. But as Ricento and Hornberger (1996) point out, "policies change as they move down the administrative levels, either explicitly in new written documents or through interpretation of existing documents" (p. 417). In this instance, the federal metrics do not reconcile with the lived realities of the children, youth, and families' experiences and schooling. Such policy interpretations include the key objectives outlined in California's CNA, which addresses the overall goal for all Migrant Education programs, which is to "ensure that all migrant

102 *Cristina Alfaro et al.*

students reach challenging academic standards and graduate with a high school diploma (or complete a GED) that prepares them for responsible citizenship, further learning, and productive employment" (U.S. Department of Education, 2016b). We argue that while it is important to consider academic achievement and success, the required reported metrics remain disconnected from the true educational experiences of the migrant children and youth. Thus, the question remains, how do the four GPRA measures address the first goal of the CNA that indicates that migrant students should not be penalized for *disparities among curriculum, graduation requirements, or academic content?* To this end, for example, when collecting and reporting graduation rates, does this metric in fact tell the full story of how students are achieving in school? We will now consider the overall emotional and physical health and well-being of migrant children as a necessary precursor to academic achievement.

The Inner Layer: Cultural Wealth and Transformative Measures of Success

To address the inner layer of the "onion metaphor," we apply Yosso's cultural wealth model as a point of departure to juxtapose the outer layer of policy with the inner layer of an authentic approach. This shifts the deficit paradigm to an approach based on critical hope with an understanding for shifting educators' critical consciousness. We postulate that this approach be considered in policy, where too often mandates focus on deficits such as: low SES, language deficits, and mobility factors. While seven forms of cultural wealth or "capital" are identified by Yosso (2005), we consider six for possible metrics of success for migrant children and youth:

1 *Aspirational capital* refers to the ability to maintain hopes and dreams despite real and perceived barriers.
2 *Linguistic capital* refers to intellectual and social skills attained through communication experiences in more than one language and/or style, such as translating and interpreting abilities, creative storytelling, and other "oral culture" skills.
3 *Familial capital* refers to forms of knowledge nurtured among family members, such as *dichos* or proverbs, *consejos* or advice, *cuentos* or stories.
4 *Social capital* refers to networks of people and community resources that can help students navigate school and other institutions.
5 *Navigational capital* refers to student resilience coupled with support networks that help students persist.
6 *Resistance capital* refers to knowledge and skills developed in opposition to mistreatment and unfair treatment.

These six forms of cultural wealth identify strengths specific to Latino students and challenge dominant deficit perspectives of Latino students and migrant communities. This may appear to be disconnected from the policy discussion above; however, it is critical to postulate such a narrative at this juncture as a point of reflection and consideration as to how norms are viewed and valued within a policy arena as we move towards the inner layer of student voices, teacher experience, and lived realities.

Progressive educators, researchers, and theorists have long argued that approaches to education reform that do not honor the cultural and linguistic resources of Latinos are likely to fail (Portes, Salas, Baquedano-López, & Mellom, 2013; Valencia, 2010; Yosso, 2005). In the field of education, short-term technical responses in the form of policy, pre-packaged curricula or lockstep methodologies, and assessments have typically been the educational norm, as illustrated above in the Title I, Title III, and more specifically the Migrant Education Program under Title I Part C. Thus it is imperative for us, as critical educators, to discern that there are no easy answers, no supernatural educational accountability measures, methods, or curricula that will magically transform low-SES, non-standard language speakers into middle-class achievers (Alfaro & Bartolomé, in press). Groundbreaking research that challenges worn-out deficit views of working class migrant youth and embraces a "cultural wealth" view of these students offers us fresh hope that the aspirational, resistance, cultural, and linguistic capital our migrant youth bring to school will be acknowledged along with other forms of nonmonetary capital (Darder, 2012; Hollins, 2014; Nieto, 2010; Pérez Huber, 2009; Solórzano & Yosso, 2000; Yosso, 2005).

Our recent engagement and conversations with migrant youth and teachers framed around a cultural wealth approach have begun to identify the critical conditions that support students' success in school. While these may not "reform" current educational accountability measures, we hope they will spark a discussion towards more transformative and cultural wealth models for educating migrant children and youth.

The Core/Heart: Migrant Youth Critical Voices

> Me gustaría que mis maestros comprendieran que además de ser un estudiante de secundaria, yo trabajo en el campo todos los días incluyendo fines de semana. Cuando mis maestros me preguntan "¿por qué no hiciste tu tarea?"—no sé qué decir porque dudo que van a entender. (I would like for my teachers to grasp that in addition to being a high school student, I work in the field everyday including weekends. When my teachers ask me "why didn't you complete your homework?" I do not know what to say because I doubt that they will understand.)
>
> (Nacho,[3] 8th grade migrant student)

Nacho's quote eloquently describes how migrant youth in the U.S. have historically suffered from a lack of understanding by mainstream teachers because their lives are not mainstream or "normal." Migrant youth and their often non-conventional English or native language(s) among low socioeconomic status linguistic minority students, the majority of whom are

104 *Cristina Alfaro et al.*

from Latino descent, have generally been viewed as deficient with a need to be fixed. As was pointed out previously, "Latino migrant students continue to face a multitude of challenges that go beyond the everyday challenges of students from non-migrant families" (Zavala, Pérez, González, & Díaz Villela, 2014, p. 2). Further, "migrant students are among the populations least likely to attend higher education" (Zavala et al., 2014, p. 3).

Given California's large Latino migrant population, the cultural and linguistic characteristics of the community funds of knowledge remain a central construct to understanding resulting classroom practices and community interactions (González, Moll, & Amanti, 2005). Romo and Chavez (2006) characterize the borderland as a hybrid space in which individuals are constantly negotiating multiple languages and identities: "the geopolitical border between Mexico and United States represents the beginnings, endings, and blending of languages, cultures, communities, and countries" (p. 142). In their work on border pedagogy, Cline and Necochea (2006) have argued that teachers working in borderland communities require certain dispositions in order to appropriately serve their students. These dispositions are the foundation for a teacher's development of ideological clarity. Teaching and designing instruction for students in these contexts consequently raises a number of issues and challenges that are specific to the complex relationships between socioeconomic status, race, culture, and language in migrant communities, especially those that find themselves at "*la frontera.*" The *testimonios* that follow describe recurring themes that illustrate elements drawn from Yosso's (2005) Cultural Wealth Model, and as such have made the educational engagement of these youth possible and filled with some level of critical hope.

Developing Familial and Social Relationships

> A turning point for me was when my teacher came to visit my family, in our humble surroundings, to share a cup of coffee around a conversation about how we could all work together so that I can go to college. She told my parents that I was extremely smart and had a bright future ahead of me—if we all worked together, like a family.
>
> (Claudia, 10th grade migrant student)

Claudia's statement depicts how a simple gesture from a teacher that notices a student's talents and strengths from a cultural wealth perspective has helped her family procure the cultural capital to gain access to higher education. In Claudia's case, her parents work in the field and reside far from the school and do not own a car for transportation. As a result, they were not able to attend the scheduled parent-teacher conference at her high school. However, Claudia's parents were extremely pleased when her teacher visited them in their home to share the good news about how to plan for college now that she is in the 10th grade and doing well in school. This was especially critical since her parents only have a 6th grade education and she is the oldest of four children. From a familial perspective, Claudia's parents felt valued due to the *respeto* and *cariño* (respect and love) in her teacher's approach towards her family. This illustrates the positive concepts of social and familial interactions, and how the involvement and commitment on the part of a caring educator, as well as the trust and respect the family has for Claudia, in that she felt safe to bring the teacher into her home knowing her parents would be accepting. Given this authentic respect and care demonstrated by her teacher, Claudia and her family have begun to plan together for her university pathway.

Navigating Trauma, Stress, and Outside Responsibilities

> I came to the United States in search for work to help my family back home in Guatemala; consequently I was picked up by the border patrol and informed that because I was an unaccompanied minor I would need to enroll in school. This came as a complete shock to me.
>
> (Valentino, 11th grade migrant student)

Valentino's story is one that for the first five months of the year was unknown to his teachers and school administration. He was assigned to an 11th grade "English Only" environment without any support system. He speaks Xinca, his indigenous language, Spanish, and recently began to learn English in the most traumatic manner (i.e., sink or swim). Here Valentino illustrates his linguistic capital, as he navigated multiple languages, while he also feared deportation on any given day. An area that is understudied in migrant education is the effect of the toxic stress that can occur due to "excessive or prolonged activation of stress response systems in the body and brain" (Center on the Developing Child, 2016, para. 1). When there is fear of deportation, this additional stress factor can impact overall health and well-being.

Valentino illustrated navigational capital in that he demonstrated resiliency by identifying support networks and individuals who were and are still working with him. He did this while he suffered complex trauma every day as he worked in the fields, attended school as much as possible, and worried about not making enough money to sustain himself and also send survival money to his family back home. Things were not looking good for Valentino until one day when his teacher, Miss Joya, met him while he sat alone having lunch. She immediately took interest in his linguistic capital and his migratory living conditions and way of life. Miss Joya spoke with the school administration to have Valentino moved to her 10th grade English class, where she was able to help him with reading and writing in academics while at the same time navigate between his home and school culture. As of this writing, this teacher has been an advocate and resource for him in finding legal assistance, trauma counseling, and academic support. As Harvard's Center on the Developing Child (2016) reports,

106   Cristina Alfaro et al.

programs or services can remediate the conditions or provide stable, buffering relationships with adult caregivers. Research shows that, even under stressful conditions, supportive, responsive relationships with caring adults as early in life as possible can prevent or reverse the damaging effects of toxic stress response.

(para. 7)

Aspirational Courage, Social Capital, and Revolutionary Love

> When I told my teacher my story and why I was not completing my work she told me "my success is her success and we are going to fight to be successful together." At this moment I felt this "fierce love" and compassion from my teacher that gave me the hope I need[ed].
>
> (Marcos, 9th grade migrant student)

What Marcos describes in this quote is the type of teacher that listened, noticed, and cared. Marcos goes on to say "she truly gets it." Marcos migrated to California from Mexico at the age of 12 and is currently in the 9th grade. He comes from a single parent family; his dad was deported two years ago, and his mother works in the field to support him and his younger brother. He has taken on the role of taking care of his brother and looking after his mother's well-being. Given these responsibilities, he was struggling academically and was actually considering dropping out of school to work full-time. He had lost hope in pursuing his education. Fortunately, he met Miss Joya, who became his advocate and transformed his path. Marcos is no longer considering dropping out of school and has begun to develop critical hope within the educational process. When a teacher is able to learn their migrant students' stories, they are then able to use this as both a resource and an asset to arm their revolutionary love (Darder, 2014; Duncan-Andrade & Morrell, 2008; Freire, 1993). It is this revolutionary love "that is strong enough to bring about radical change in individual students, classrooms, school systems, and the larger society that controls them" (Duncan-Andrade & Morrell, 2008, p. 187).

Cultural Wealth and Ideological Clarity

> My students and their families know that I have high expectations for them and that they can expect high support from me. In order to guide my migrant students to reach these high expectations, I build on their funds of knowledge— I honor who they are and where they come from by creating a relevant and purposeful curriculum coupled with appropriate pedagogy.
>
> (Paloma, high school teacher)

This quote eloquently describes the ideological clarity and varying elements of the cultural wealth approach Paloma employs in her work with migrant youth. She does this to ensure that her students receive a culturally

Navigating Politics, Access, and Equity 107

and linguistically relevant education with high expectations and support. Although no research definitively links teachers' ideological stances with particular instructional practices, many scholars have suggested that teachers' ideological orientations are often reflected in their beliefs and attitudes and in the way they interact with students in the classroom (Alfaro & Bartolomé, in press; Cochran-Smith, 2004; Hollins, 2014; Macedo, 2015; Marx, 2006; Marx & Pennington, 2003; Nieto, 2010; Sleeter, 1993).

In this case, Paloma possesses a well-articulated ideological stance that guides her in navigating the political agendas she encounters in her work with migrant youth and their families. Paloma authentically understands that her work with migrant students must go beyond academics in order to engage her students *con respeto* (with respect). Previous research has established the importance of a "facilitative social environment" where the teacher is

> ... key not only in organizing the social uses and practices of language(s), both oral and written across social contexts, but also in the type of social interactions, socio-cultural rituals, expectations, and *respeto* (respect) that become the ways of knowing, the ways of being, the ways of acting, the ways of doing, and the ways of socially interacting in the classroom.
>
> (Flores, 2007, p. 34, emphasis in original)

These stories of migrant youth and their teachers illustrate the cultural wealth approach as a critical race theory challenge to traditional interpretations of cultural capital. These forms of cultural wealth draw on and acknowledge what migrant youth bring with them from their homes and communities into the classroom. A cultural wealth approach to migrant education involves a commitment to developing schools that acknowledge students' multiple strengths and funds of knowledge in order to serve a larger purpose towards equity and social justice (Alfaro & Hernández, 2016).

Conclusions and Implications

As the student voices illustrate, and we argue, it is incumbent upon educators to embrace a cultural wealth model that shifts the research lens away from a deficit view of migrant communities as places full of cultural poverty, disadvantages, and low academic achievement, and instead focuses on and learns from the array of existent cultural knowledge, skills, abilities, and contacts possessed by migrant communities that often go unrecognized and unacknowledged. How then do we measure the *heart* that exists within federal and state mandates, the outer layers of policy, with a focus on the results of reading, math, and graduation rates? We recommend that rather than simply mandating policies and standards, we create transformative institutional networks, designed to ensure the success of migrant youth in our educational

108 *Cristina Alfaro et al.*

system. These networks, the inner layers connecting policy to the core, can include support systems, such as learning communities with culturally efficacious educators (Bustos Flores, Claeys, Gist, Riojas Clark, & Villarreal, 2015; Quezada, Rodríguez-Valls, and Lindsey, this volume). They can support practices based on Yosso's (2005) cultural wealth model, which hold promise in supporting and advocating for historically marginalized student populations. To this end, it is incumbent upon policymakers and educators at all levels to strategically and creatively seek out efforts to promote richer definitions of success for individuals and develop a continuity of education for migrant children that fosters educators' cultural and linguistic efficaciousness (Bustos Flores et al., 2015). This requires educators to work along with policymakers to advocate for cultural and linguistic values of migrant communities and further design policy that aligns funding with measurable authentic priorities. By the very nature of migrant students' mobility, migrant students are directly and indirectly impacted by the variance in state education programs and requirements.

At the same time, we acknowledge the difficulties and hardships that arise due to high mobility resulting from seeking work opportunities for survival. We recognize that students are unable to thrive if their basic needs go unmet. We consider how a focus on educational metrics of measuring academic success can blatantly ignore the lived experiences of migrant students and their families and specifically their emotional and overall well-being that must be addressed before any discussion of academics should occur. Thus, health and well-being of migrant students should be a larger priority than academics; they will be more prepared for school when their basic needs are met; the necessary conditions for migrant student success are not only academics, but also social, physical, and emotional health. Migrant student success requires attention to the needs of the whole student. Given this, it is incumbent upon those of us working with migrant populations to investigate where there are programs in place that support whole student's well-being by conducting a community scan (Ochoa, 2009) and considering the following questions. Where are there wraparound services or full-service community schools in place? Where are there existing partnerships between schools and communities? Where these programs exist, how well are they working? Deliberate on how we might work with stakeholders to support, build upon, and heighten the work that is currently being engaged. Finally, consider visiting a school district with wraparound or community school strategies in place to examine the goals and outcomes of these existing programs (Community Schools Research, 2009).

In the end, we concur with the California MEP as reported by the Legislative Analyst Office (2006) that to help reduce the educational disruptions that result from repeated relocations, we must:

- provide coordinated educational and support services;
- ensure migrant children who move among the states are not adversely affected by differences in state education programs or requirements;

Navigating Politics, Access, and Equity   109

- ensure migrant students are exposed to the same academic content and held to the same achievement standards as other children;
- and prepare migrant students to make a successful transition to postsecondary education or employment.

If and when educational institutions and agencies strategically focus on the above four points articulated by MEP—through a cultural wealth model (Yosso, 2005)—a social justice/counter-hegemonic educational paradigm will have the potential to advance for the benefit of migrant children and youth. This counter-hegemonic paradigm can position educators and policymakers, with the heart of the issues, to collectively embrace migrant students' historical cultural and linguistic backgrounds, lived experiences, perspectives, voices, struggles, and their emerging cultural formations (hooks, 1994), thus transforming to a space and time where migrant students and their families' reality are no longer invisible.

Notes

1 Mini Corps is unique to California, is funded by Migrant Education as a program for undergraduate students who identify as former migrant students and are employed as teacher assistants in migrant impacted summer schools.
2 Replaced in 2015 with Smarter Balanced Assessment System.
3 Pseudonyms are used for student and teacher names.

References

Alfaro, C. & Bartolomé, L. I. (In Press). La claridad ideológica del maestro bilingüe: Un reto en la educación bilingüe de calidad. In M. Guerrero, L. Soltero-González, C. Guerrero & K. Escamilla (Eds.), *Los fundamentos de la educacion bilingue. Dual Language Education.* New Mexico. Albuquerque, NM: Fuente Press.

Alfaro, C. & Hernández, A. M. (2016). Ideology, pedagogy, access, and equity (IPAE): A critical examination for dual language educators. In *Multilingual Educator*, Covina, CA: California Association for Bilingual Education Conference Edition (pp. 6–9).

Borre, K., Ertle, L. & Graff, M. (2010) Working to eat: Vulnerability, food insecurity, and obesity among migrant and seasonal farmworker families. *American Journal of Industrial Medicine, 53*(4), 443–462.

Branz-Spall, A. M. & Rosenthal, R. (with Wright, A.). (2003). Children of the road: Migrant students, our nation's most mobile population. *Journal of Negro Education, 72,* 55–62.

Bustos Flores, B. (2016, April). *Ensuring bilingual candidates' Spanish language proficiency as a democratic principle.* Paper presented at the annual meeting of the American Education Research Association, Washington, DC.

Bustos Flores, B., Claeys, L., Gist, C., Riojas Clark, E. & Villarreal, A. (2015). Culturally efficacious mathematics and science teacher preparation for working with English learners. *Teacher Education Quarterly, 42*(4), 3–31.

California Department of Education. (2007). California migrant education program comprehensive needs assessment [document]. Retrieved from http://www.cde. ca.gov/sp/me/mt/needsassessment.asp

110 Cristina Alfaro et al.

California Department of Education. (2012). California migrant education program state service delivery plan [document]. Retrieved from http://www.cde.ca.gov/sp/me/mt/ssdp.asp

California Department of Education. (2016a). Migrant education program overview. Retrieved from http://www.cde.ca.gov/sp/me/mt/overview.asp

California Department of Education. (2016b). Title I overview. Retrieved from http://www.cde.ca.gov/sp/sw/t1/titleparta.asp

California Department of Education. (2016c). Title III overview. Retrieved from http://www.cde.ca.gov/sp/el/t3/title3faq.asp

Center on the Developing Child, Harvard University. (2016). Key concepts: Toxic stress. *The President and Fellows of Harvard College*. Retrieved from http://developingchild.harvard.edu/science/key-concepts/toxic-stress/

Cline, Z. & Necochea, J. (2006). Teacher dispositions for effective education in the borderlands. *The Educational Forum, 70*(3), 268–282.

Cochran-Smith, M. (2004). *Walking the road: Race, diversity and social justice in teacher education*. New York: Teachers College Press.

Community Schools Research Brief 09. (2009). Accessed at results section, coalition for community schools web site. Retrieved from www.communityschools.org/assets/

Darder, A. (2012). *Culture and power in the classroom: Educational foundations for the schooling of bicultural students*. New York: Paradigm Publishers.

Darder, A. (2014). *Freire and education*. New York: Routledge.

Duncan-Andrade, J. M. R. & Morrell, E. (2008). *The art of critical pedagogy: Possibilities for moving from theory to practice in urban schools* (Vol. 285). New York: Peter Lang.

Farmworker Justice. (2013). *Exposed and ignored: How pesticides are endangering our nation's farmworkers*. Washington, DC: Author.

Flores, B. (2007). Biliteracy as social practice in schooling: Bilingual first grader's journey in learning to read and write in L1 and L2. In Y. Goodman and P. Martens (Eds.), *Critical issues in early literacy: Research and pedagogy* (pp. 31–45). New York: Routledge.

Freire, P. (1993). *Pedagogy of the city*. New York: Continuum.

González, N., Moll, L. & Amanti, C. (2005). *Funds of knowledge: Theorizing practices in households, communities and classrooms*. Mahwah, NJ: Lawrence Erlbaum.

Green, P. E. (2003). The undocumented: Educating the children of migrant workers in America. *Bilingual Research Journal, 27*(1), 51–71.

Hill, L. & Hayes, J. (2007). *Out of school immigrant youth*. San Francisco, CA: Public Policy Institute. Retrieved from http://www.ppic.org/content/pubs/report/R_407LHR.pdf

Hollins, E. (2014). *Culture in school learning: Revealing the deep meaning*, Third Edition. New York: Routledge.

hooks, b. (1994). *Teaching to transgress: Education as the practice of freedom*. New York: Routledge.

Hornberger, N. H. & Johnson, D. C. (2007). Slicing the onion ethnographically: Layers and spaces in multilingual language education policy and practice. *TESOL Quarterly, 41*(3), 509–532.

Kandel, W. (2008). *Profile of hired farmworkers, a 2008 update* (Economic Research Report Number 60) [Electronic version]. Washington, DC: Economic Research Service, United States Department of Agriculture. Retrieved from http://digitalcommons.ilr.cornell.edu/key_workplace/559/

Kindler, A. L. (2002). Migrants, education of. *Encyclopedia of Education*. Retrieved from http://www.encyclopedia.com/doc/1G2–3403200409.html

LaCroix, C. (2007). Girls and boys, interrupted: Working to fill gaps in migrant students' education. *Edutopia*. Retrieved from http://www.edutopia.org/girls-boys-interrupted

Legislative Analyst Office. (2006). *Improving services for migrant students*. Retrieved from http://www.lao.ca.gov/2006/migrant_ed/migrant_education_021506.htm

Lopez, G. R. (2001). The value of hard work: Lessons on parent involvement from (im)migrant household. *Harvard Educational Review, 71*(3), 416–437.

Lopez, G. R. (2004). Bringing the mountain to Mohammed: Parent involvement in migrant-impacted schools. In C. Salinas & M. Fránquiz (Eds.), *Scholars in the field: The challenges of migrant education* (pp. 135–146). Charleston, WV: ERIC Clearinghouse on Rural Education and Small Schools.

Lundy-Ponce, G. (2010). Migrant students: What we need to know to help them succeed. *Colorin Colorado* website. Retrieved May 10, 2016 from http://www.colorincolorado.org/article/migrant-students-what-we-need-know-help-them-succeed

Macedo, D. (2015, February 12). Personal communication.

Marx, S. (2006). *Revealing the invisible: Confronting passive racism in teacher education*. New York: Routledge.

Marx, S. & Pennington, J. (2003). Pedagogies of critical race theory: Experimentations with White preservice teachers. *International Journal of Qualitative Studies in Education, 16*(1), 91–110.

Nieto, S. (2010). *Language, culture, and teaching: Critical perspectives* (Vol. 2). New York: Routledge.

Ochoa, A. M. (2009). Community profile: Understanding the diversity of a school community. Updated from source: A. M. Ochoa & I. River (Eds.), (1978). Planning and Implementing Issues in Bilingual Education Programming. Manual for the Institute for Cultural Pluralism, No. V, San Diego State University.

Pérez Huber, L. (2009). Challenging racist nativist framing: Acknowledging the community cultural wealth of undocumented Chicana college students to reframe the immigration debate. *Harvard Educational Review, 79*(4), 704–730.

Portes, P., Salas, S., Baquedano-López, P. & Mellom, P. (Eds.) (2013). *U.S. Latinos and education policy: Research-based directions for change*. New York: Routledge.

Relano Pastor, A. M. (2007). On border identities. 'Transfronterizo' students in San Diego. *Diskurs Kindheits-und Jugendforschung, 2*(3), 263–277.

Ricento, T. K. & Hornberger, N. H. (1996). Unpeeling the onion: Language planning and policy and the ELT professional. *TESOL Quarterly, 30*(3), 401–427.

Romo, J. J. & Chavez, C. (2006). Border pedagogy: A study of preservice teacher transformation. *The Educational Forum, 70*(2), 142–153.

Rosaldo, R. (1989). *Culture & truth: The remaking of social analysis*. Boston: Beacon Press.

Salinas, C. & Franquiz, M. E. (2004). *Scholars in the field: The challenges of migrant education*. Charleston, WV: AEL.

Sleeter, C. E. (1993). How White teachers construct race. In C. McCarthy & W. Crichlow (Eds.), *Race identity and representation in education* (pp. 157–171). New York: Routledge.

Solis, J. (2004). Scholastic demands on intrastate and interstate migrant secondary students. In C. Salinas & M. E. Fránquiz (Eds.), *Scholars in the field: The*

112 *Cristina Alfaro et al.*

challenges of migrant education (pp. 113–117). Charleston, WV: ERIC Clearinghouse on Rural Education and Small Schools.

Solórzano, D. G. & Yosso, T. J. (2000). Maintaining social justice hopes within academic realities: A Freirean approach to critical race/LatCrit pedagogy. *Denver University Law Review, 78*(4), 595–621.

Suárez-Orozco, M. M., Suárez-Orozco, C. & Sattin-Bajaj, C. (2010). Making migration work. *Peabody Journal of Education, 85*(4), 535–551.

U.S. Department of Education. (2015). Every student succeeds act. Retrieved from http://www.ed.gov/essa?src=rn

U.S. Department of Education. (2016a). *Education Data Express.* Retrieved from http://eddataexpress.ed.gov/

U.S. Department of Education. (2016b). *Migrant education program basic state formula grants.* Retrieved from http://www2.ed.gov/programs/mep/index.html

Valencia, R. R. (2010). *Dismantling contemporary deficit thinking: Educational thought and practice.* New York: Routledge.

Yosso, T. J. (2005). Whose culture has capital? A critical race theory discussion of community cultural wealth. *Race, Ethnicity, and Education, 8*(1), 69–91.

Zalaquett, C. P., Alvarez McHatton, P. & Cranston-Gingras, A. (2007). Characteristics of Latina/o migrant farmworker students attending a large metropolitan university. *Journal of Hispanic Higher Education, 6*(2), 135–156.

Zavala, M., Pérez, P. A., González, A. & Díaz Villela, A. (2014). Con Respeto: A conceptual model for building healthy community-university partnerships alongside Mexican migrant families. *Journal of Critical Thought and Praxis, 3*(2), 1–31.

8 From the Fields to Fieldwork

Cuentos from the Daughter of
Migrant Farmworkers

Ebelia Hernández

I wish I could say that I have a secret formula for success in academia. I don't. In fact, I have struggled to think of how to write my story about a childhood in the rural agricultural lands of California to the halls of a well-known university in the East as a professor. I am not special. I am not exceptional. I am not being humble. This is the truth. I cannot compare my educational story to those of other Latinos and Latinas, such as Laura Rendón (1992) in her essay on being a scholarship girl, Ruben Navarrette (1994) and his experience as a Chicano at Harvard, or Richard Rodriguez (1983) in his account of reaching the most elite scholarly circles only to leave it for a new life.

However, I have my own *cuentos* (stories) of being a less than exceptional student, often invisible and overlooked. *Cuentos*, a form of storytelling, are ways that Latinos pass on their knowledge, history, and wisdom to others (Yosso, 2005). They are *cuentos* of mistakes with hopes of teaching a lesson of what not to do. *Cuentos* convey hope and aspirations for the future. The *cuentos* I relate here are of my family's search for the American Dream. They reveal my family's history: our migration from Mexico to various parts of the U.S., our experiences as agricultural workers in California, and how our hopes for a better future led to who I am today. These *cuentos* illustrate the yearning my parents had for education and the life that I kept hidden from my classmates in order to minimize how different we were, but I feel compelled to share now to help educators understand many of the experiences that I share with other children of migrant farmworkers.

Opportunity to Learn

My mother and father grew up in a village in central Mexico called Tingambato. It was the kind of place where the men went with their *burros* to tend to their crops of beans and corn in the morning, and the women walked to the *molino* (mill) to grind their *nixtamal* into tortilla dough and then set themselves to the work of making tortillas for the day. Children went to school as long as their families could afford it. Families had to pay for their children's books, pencils, uniforms, and even contribute to a pool of funds

114 *Ebelia Hernández*

to maintain the classroom. My father was an exceptional student with a good head for numbers, but he came from a very poor family that struggled to put food on the table. Once he finished 5th grade, my grandfather said that was enough education and it was time to work like a man. When my father stopped going to school, his teacher came to the house to see what was going on. My grandfather told him it was none of his business and ran him off despite the teacher's pleas to keep my father in school because he was his best student. My father said, "My teacher knew I had a lot of potential, but your grandfather didn't care. Imagine what I could have done if he let me go to school." I could feel sadness, bitterness, and yearning in his voice.

My father learned things on his own. He couldn't afford to keep paying a mechanic to fix the family car. He bought Chilton auto repair manuals and figured out how to keep the car from falling apart. These books were special, as they were some of the few books that existed in the family household. It didn't need to be said that daddy's Chilton books were off limits. Yet, I remember being a young girl and secretly cracking them open when he wasn't around. I wondered how could my father read these huge, thick books if he could not speak, read, or write well in English. But then I, a native English speaker and good student, realized I had no advantage because these books were full of diagrams and figures I couldn't understand.

My mother only completed her education up to the 2nd grade. She says she has a *cabeza de piedra* where knowledge just doesn't seem to sink in to her brain, but she is glad none of her children inherited this difficulty in learning. Mama, the oldest of 10 children, left school to help her mother raise her younger siblings. She told me that the moment she decided to follow my father to *el norte* was when my oldest brother was old enough to start kindergarten. For my mother, the sacrifice of leaving their village to make a new life in the U.S. was worth it because she could raise her children in a place where they could all go to school for free.

Cana

I hated it when the lights would flash on in the bedroom early on Saturday mornings. "*Vístensen, nos vamos a Cana* (Get dressed, we are going to Cana)," my father would command. A day of working with my father, big brother, and sister for the small family firewood business was not my idea of fun. It was going to be a long, hard day of work and no Saturday morning cartoons. I shoved my bad attitude and unhappiness far down. No one else complained or dared tell my father they didn't want to go to work. My parents never complained of working hard, so who was I to gripe about working a few days a week? Even though I was a just a skinny adolescent girl in junior high, I knew I had the responsibility to contribute to the family too.

My resentment slowly melted away to resignation as the sun rose in the sky. It was a good hour's drive to the almond orchards where my dad and brother would cut down trees and my sister and I would move the brush and toss the newly cut logs into the trailer. After our muscles warmed up to the work and we were well into the midmorning, my attitude warmed up too. My sister and I joked with each other, and my brother did us the favor of turning on the radio to listen to top-40 American music. Sure, I had the weakest arms and seemed to be the most affected by the heat, but I didn't stop working slow and steady. I was called *Tortuga* (turtle), but I finished my workday just like everybody else. The best part of the day was stopping at the quickie mart on our way home for our very own fountain drink. My parents didn't usually indulge us with buying fountain drinks, much less one that we didn't have to share sips with another sibling, but we earned the treat of a cold drink from working a full day.

There was honor and pride in working in the orchards. I felt good to contribute and fulfill my obligation to my family. Of course, we never talked about pride or family obligation, just like my parents never complained of the sore muscles and general fatigue of being farmworkers. Work was just part of living.

My mother wanted more for me. She wanted me to get out of the fields and get a job where I could use my head rather than my muscles. She dreamed of me being a secretary so I could go to work in a nice office where it would be clean and air-conditioned. I could go to work looking like a professional lady instead of my farm laborer uniform of hat, pants, and long-sleeved shirts to protect my body from the sun, bugs, and scratches from tree branches. Because I knew how to speak English well, and I could read and write, she believed I had a real chance of leaving the fields for an office job so long as I applied myself to my studies.

When I neared high school graduation, my parents gave me two options. One, become an adult and get a full-time job, probably not in an office because a high school degree would not be enough to be a professional lady. Or, two, go to college. I chose to go to college. My father could not afford to help me pay tuition but he gave me a car to commute to school. I didn't realize until much later that the car was my reward for all those mornings of going to Cana.

GATE

When I was in the second grade, I was pulled out of class to the portable classrooms located on the far side of the school. A nice lady sat me down and asked me to play with red and white blocks. The game was for me to copy the designs she had on a piece of paper with the colored blocks. She also asked me questions about words that I hadn't heard before. "What does this word mean?," she would ask. "I'm not sure. Can you tell me?," I would reply. She chuckled, and replied that it was my job to figure it out. It didn't seem like it was necessary for anyone to tell me who this lady was, nor why I was playing these silly games. I ended up testing into GATE

116 *Ebelia Hernández*

(Gifted and Talented Education). When my mother asked me if I wanted to go to special classes, I said yes because I was excited about the possibility of getting out of regular class to do more silly puzzles.

I sat quietly in the GATE classroom with the students I considered to be the rich, White kids in my grade. There were no other Mexicans in GATE. There were no Black kids either, as we didn't have any in the entire school district. We did our logic puzzles. We did our SAT test preparatory questions. I participated to some extent, but wondered if I was really welcomed there. Was GATE a group of the smartest kids in school? If so, why was I there? I wasn't in the highest reading group (why I, a second grader would be aware of this truth is interesting, and even more interesting was how much I felt that I really belonged in the higher reading group).

As the years went by, the other kids I hung around with (i.e., those who ended up taking college preparatory courses like me), also tested for GATE but did not get in: my best friend who was constantly on the honor roll and was a much better writer than me, another friend who was also a good student and one of the best athletes, and the boy who ended up being the class valedictorian. I heard that some parents asked for their children to be tested, but even parental recommendation couldn't ensure a spot in that special classroom if they didn't pass that test. I wondered if I was the token brown kid, but if so, they could have had a better representative for the Mexicans. There was that other Mexican girl (who would grow up to be a doctor) who got better grades than me. She wasn't the child of farmworkers, and she had a middle-class lifestyle that was much more like the GATE kids. I heard she invited them all to her birthday party at her home once. Interestingly, she was tested too and didn't get in. Every time another classmate shared they didn't get into GATE, I wondered if they also questioned how the heck I got in. I felt like the guest who got in to an exclusive party after having to show proof of invitation to get in—I had the right to be there, but I never felt like I was welcomed.

Perhaps I had an exceptional talent. One student in GATE could listen to music and then play it on the piano. Another student was great at drawing and ended up winning Best of Show for her art project at the State Fair. Another was a great dancer. What was my exceptional talent? I liked to draw but I was astute enough to know I was not exceptional. My siblings teased me for using "five dollar words" in my everyday talk, but a large vocabulary was considered more of a defect of my incurable dorkiness than a talent. I could not identify any significant gift or talent that merited my place in GATE.

Yet, despite feeling like the unwelcomed guest in my GATE class, I knew I belonged. I knew I was just as smart (if not smarter) as the other kids despite not being placed automatically in the highest academic tracks. I also knew I was talented, but I could not name my talents until I was almost 30 years old in graduate school. The test was not wrong after all.

Migration

My grandfather, Jesus, was a participant in the *Bracero* Program. From about 1942 to 1964, the U.S. government provided temporary work visas to Mexican men to help with the harvest season. He left his young, pregnant wife in their tiny village to work in Texas, Oklahoma, and several states in the south. My grandmother, Salud, hearing the rumor that he had found himself another woman, followed him to *el norte*. The result was her personally finding out the falseness of the rumor as well as giving birth to my mother, Ines, in El Indio, Texas. Salud returned back to Mexico to raise the family, and my grandfather came back to the U.S. for the harvest season a few more times over the years.

My mother and father grew up in the same village. When my mother was almost 16, they eloped. My father had little education and no family lands to farm to support a new wife. It seemed like his only option to make a living was to go to *el norte*. Like my grandfather, he too worked in the fields across the south, following the work from harvest to harvest. He roomed with other migrant men in small apartments. It was no place for a woman, as the men moved in groups from one place to another, living like bachelors with only the bare necessities to get them by. My father told me that he offered to do laundry for the guy who worked in a restaurant in exchange for food. My father did what he could to survive and make as much money as he could to send back to my mother.

My father made it to northern California in the early 1970s and found a small farming community where he saw a few other Mexican migrant men who had settled down with their families. Back in those days, there were very few Mexicans in this particular part of California and little cultural connections to make it more welcoming. There were no Spanish language radio stations or access to channels in Spanish, so he got to know The Carpenters, Carole King, and Frank Sinatra, as well as the Waltons, Little Joe and Hoss, and the good ol' boys from the Dukes of Hazzard. He stopped following the work in the fields when he got a job working at a dairy farm, and then later he got a job working for an almond grower. His boss gave him a house to live in so he could manage the surrounding orchards year round. My childhood was spent living in those almond orchards where we paired the yearly cycle of seasons with phases of the almond tree.

More men from the village followed my father to California to work in the almond orchards. They dreamed of an America where they could make a lot of dollars to send back to their families, and to have a taste of the life of luxury that they assumed all Americans had. They didn't realize that the reality of life for migrant farmworkers was much harder. Some couldn't overcome the homesickness, discrimination, fear of deportation, or how hard it would be on the body to work the harvest season. Many would barely last one harvest and the sweltering heat that often would reach over

118 *Ebelia Hernández*

100 degrees, and would never come back. A few endured and came back for several harvest seasons, making small fortunes to build a house or send children to school. A smaller number of men found permanent work that allowed them to bring their wives and raise their children in California.

While my family was no longer living the life of a migrant farmworker, our close connections with these recent immigrants kept us in this world. My father helped the men find jobs and taught the newcomers how to work in the fields. My mother shared whatever information she knew with the wives on how to raise their children in the U.S. despite not knowing how to speak, read, or write in English. She belonged to a special network of women that helped each other learn how to enroll their children in Head Start, a federally supported preschool for low income children, sign up their kids for free lunch at school, and access family planning and prenatal care, among other things.

My siblings continued the family tradition of migration from one place to another to find opportunity. At 18 years old, my big brother packed his Toyota Celica and drove down to Los Angeles to go to college. The plan was for him to be taken in by his godparents for a while, and then find a job and make his own way. In one of her rare calls to Mexico, my mother cried over the phone to my grandfather because she missed my big brother so much. My grandfather told her to dry her eyes as he was a man *buscando su vida*, and that it was a good thing that he was going to college and seeking a better life.

I have also migrated from one state to another. I left my family and my hometown to create a future for myself. Like them, I have followed the work to places that seemed foreign and far away from what I knew. Faculty jobs in my field are scarce, so there is not much choice in where I will go to work. In some ways, I was naïve, like those idealistic immigrants, because I didn't realize that life as an academic would include the harsh realities of homesickness, discrimination, and the fear of the unknown. But I have endured. I have survived despite seeing friends come and go—sometimes by choice and sometimes because they could not make tenure or secure a permanent position. I have found my own network of women who have shared with me how to succeed as a faculty member, and I have invited new faculty into our community of support. We lean on each other to make it in this unfamiliar land.

Going Home Again

It is a hot summer day. We are driving through Durham, California. This is where I grew up. I am not sure of the feelings that I have driving through the familiar road that takes us through the town. My sister and I comment on how pretty the park still looks, the one where we went on Easter egg hunts and had family BBQs. We drive past where I went to school from my first day of kindergarten to my last day in high school, and the feelings we have are not of sweet nostalgia, but of relief that those days are far behind use. We take the road that we used to take to walk to school, and not much has changed in 20 years.

Our road weaves between houses and almond orchards. The almonds are turning from green to brown, but they still have a good month left before harvest. The sprinklers are on in some of the orchards, and I see that some orchards still have irrigation pipes. "Yuck," I say. "I remember having to move those pipes with my sister, Maggie, after school. I hated doing that." I explain that we had to move the pipes from one lane to the other so that the attached sprinklers could irrigate a new part of the orchard the next day. Someone commented that it must have been hard work, and that it surely must have been motivation to do well in school.

More memories come to me as we continue driving through this little town. Memories of hard work and a hard life. The image I have of myself as a young girl moving pipe in the orchards—with muddy shoes and sweat on my brow—doesn't reconcile with who I am now, an elegant lady in pretty clothes going to the opening of a new winery. The people pouring me samples into my glass are friendly, yet I get that familiar feeling of being the outsider sitting in the GATE class with the rich, White kids. I have transformed to become an even better version of the professional woman my mother hoped for, but the girl that I was working in the fields has not disappeared. I cannot connect with these people as they do not know who I really am, what I have lived, what I have done despite having lived in the same small town and having sat next to them in the classroom.

The Child of Field Hands Returns to Do Fieldwork[1]

These *cuentos* share my family history and our hopes for the future. I have more family stories, but these are the ones that came to me to convey our life as farmworkers. They also tell how we viewed education as the key to getting out of poverty and finding jobs where we could use our heads rather than our hands. I cannot really tell you how my siblings and I all made it— we all went to college and have become the professional ladies and men my mom hoped we would become. How did we persevere instead of falling into despair or anger over our circumstances? Perhaps it was our certainty that education would give us opportunity. Perhaps it was the fact that uncertainty and fear are not good enough reasons to stop moving forward in life or to resist going to unknown places to find opportunity. Or, maybe it was the knowledge that the only ones who could get us out of poverty were ourselves. These were lessons we learned as children of migrant farmworkers.

These *cuentos* also share the quiet ache I had as a child of never feeling fully welcomed in school, where I was often invisible or had teachers that underestimated my intellectual curiosities and talents. It was not until I was a college student that I blossomed and found that sense of belonging and a feeling of community with other students of color who, like me, wanted

120 *Ebelia Hernández*

to find their own American Dream (Hurtado & Carter, 1997). I hope that these stories help educators consider the quiet ones in the corners as full of potential. Perhaps, like me, they stay silent because they feel out of place, not because they don't have anything to say. I challenge educators to make these students feel that they too belong in the classroom and to not take silence as disinterest or lack of understanding. I also challenge educators to be clear with students and their parents about testing so that it does not create uneasiness or confusion, such as I experienced when I was placed in GATE.

My *cuentos* are taking a different turn, as I am now a university professor who conducts research about Latinas/os in postsecondary education. I am the child of field hands who has returned to do a special kind of fieldwork. I do fieldwork in research where my job is to harvest the stories of Latinas/os in college and share with others what it is like to pursue higher education, experience the frustrations and satisfactions of being constantly tied to one's family, and the struggles and hardships of finding one's own way through life. The *cuentos* I have collected are like mine because they also share hope for a greater future for themselves and their families.

Note

1 From Ladson-Billings, G. (2003). Racialized discourses and ethnic epistemologies. In N. K. Denzin & Y. S. Lincoln (Eds.), *The landscape of qualitative research* (2nd ed., pp. 398–432, 419). Thousand Oaks, CA: Sage.

References

Hurtado, S. & Carter, D. F. (1997). Effects of college transition and perceptions of the campus racial climate on Latino college students' sense of belonging. *Sociology of Education, 70*(4), 324–345.

Navarrette, R. (1994). *A darker shade of crimson: Odyssey of a Harvard Chicano.* New York: Bantam.

Rendón, L. (1992). From the barrio to the academy: Relevations of a Mexican American "scholarship girl". *New Directions for Community Colleges, 80*, 55–64.

Rodriguez, R. (1983). *Hunger of memory: The education of Richard Rodriguez.* New York: Bantam.

Yosso, T. J. (2005). Whose culture has capital? A critical race theory discussion of community cultural wealth. *Race, Ethnicity, and Education, 8*(1), 69–91.

9 Conclusion
Future Directions for Migrant Education

Patricia A. Pérez and Maria Estela Zarate

Employing new methodological approaches and theoretical frameworks, this volume set out to contribute to the existing limited research on migrant farmworker students in the U.S. Using asset-based lenses, the authors provide data-driven solutions and strategies to improve English Language Learner development, parental involvement, college access, program design, and assessment, among other topics, all with the common goal to increase migrant student academic achievement. What is abundantly clear throughout the text is that only through quality partnerships with all stakeholders (i.e., parents, schools, personnel, teachers, etc.) can we truly make progress on student educational achievement. In the following section we offer salient lessons learned across the chapters in this volume. The final section provides future directions and guidance for Migrant Education programs, students, and families at the local, state, and federal levels.

Lessons Learned

In the Introduction, Zarate, Pérez, and Acosta situate Migrant Education programs in the evolution of federal education policies and the transnational context of globalization and migration. Zarate et al., review the primary objectives of MEP service areas and highlight existing limitations of each service area. They then prioritize salient and urgent educational challenges facing migrant farmworker students and specify current MEP policy that hinders solutions.

Cranston-Gingras and Rivera-Singletary provide an in-depth review of the three federal programs whose target population includes migrant students, including Title I, Part C (MEP), Title III (targeting English Learners), and the Individuals with Disabilities Education Act (IDEA). They argue that, collectively, these programs can expand their reach and value by collaborating when servicing migrant farmworker families. The authors highlight specific programs who have moved towards cross-program collaboration to serve migrant students and their families.

Addressing the imperative that educators of migrant children need to be prepared specifically for working with migrant families, Quezada,

122   Patricia A. Pérez and Maria Estela Zarate

Rodríguez-Valls, and Lindsey present a cultural proficiency framework to inform professional learning and collaboration. This framework contests the anonymization of migrant students in U.S. schools and challenges educators and school leaders to examine their biases, skills, knowledge, and instructional practice to truly meet the needs of migrant students.

In *"Nuestra Familia es Nuestra Fuerza,"* Jasis and González challenge deficit notions of the migrant families that place farmworker parents on the sidelines of their children's educational journeys. They document migrant parents' desire to participate in the education of their children and their hope for transformative schooling experiences. Jasis and González argue that schools and educators should seek more authentic collaboration and partnerships with migrant families to increase the impact of their programs.

In "Designing Programs to Meet and Assess the Needs of Migrant Students," authors Rodríguez-Valls and Kofford implore personnel creating programs geared towards migrant students to pay attention to the needs of migrant farmworker students and tailor programs towards those specific needs. Among the various needs of migrant student populations to be addressed include anonymization and lack of belonging. The authors highlight how the Family Biliteracy and Language Explorers programs are two key examples of such programming that have "contributed to reinforcing and strengthening college readiness and language and literacy skills." Finally, the authors also remind us that clear goals and objectives will maximize program outcomes associated with RAs and DSAs.

Among the recommendations offered by Núñez in "What Can Latina/o Migrant Students Tell us About College Outreach and Access?," the author suggests school personnel and college outreach programs offer college-planning tools and information in addition to support completing financial aid forms. Núñez also calls our attention to empowering students via development of writing skills, deconstructing deficit views of migrant students' abilities, and educating migrant students about their unique sociopolitical position in society.

> *Centering migrant students' perspectives disrupts dominant traditions of building college outreach programs that focus primarily on compensating for migrant students' perceived weaknesses and building academic, financial, and cultural resources that are typically defined by and valued in the dominant culture.*
>
> (Núñez, this volume)

Using a community cultural wealth research lens, in "Migrant Education and Shifting Consciousness: A Cultural Wealth Approach to Navigating Politics, Access, and Equity," by Alfaro, Cadiero-Kaplan, and Hernandez, the authors argue that we must center migrant student voices to learn about migrant farmworker communities. As the experts themselves, educators and researchers should "focus on and learn from the array of existent cultural knowledge, skills, abilities, and contacts possessed by migrant communities" to improve the educational opportunities and programs for migrant students. Furthermore, they suggest educators work in tandem with policymakers to facilitate efficacious and culturally relevant policy and programming that is both relevant and measurable. Relatedly, they promote learning communities taught by educators who will also serve as advocates and remind us not to ignore how social, physical, and emotional well-being are intimately tied to academic success from a holistic perspective.

Finally, in Chapter Eight, "From the Fields to Fieldwork: *Cuentos* from the Daughter of Migrant Farmworkers," Hernández intimately shares family history and her educational experiences as a daughter of migrant farmworkers and a farmworker herself toiling in the almond orchards of Durham, California. As a result of these experiences, she recommends educators reach out and try to connect with migrant students. She notes: "these students feel that they too belong in the classroom." Hernández adds that silence should not be perceived as a sign of "disinterest or lack of understanding."

Recommendations

The cross-section of research, theoretical frameworks, and programs that are presented in this volume exemplify the front line of innovation and forward-thinking in program design and frameworks for content and professional development. The implications and recommendations of each chapter can support continued improvements in service delivery. We further distilled the recommendations of each chapter to identify six common themes (see Table 9.1) and suggest actions that various administrative and

Table 9.1 Migrant Education Program Recommendations

Recommendation Goal	Program	State	Federal
Linguistic and literacy curriculum and instruction must address the unique learning, socio-cultural, and literacy development characteristics of migrant English Learner (EL) student needs.	Participate in or create professional learning communities of MEP educators to implement innovative and rigorous programs, curriculum, and instruction that addresses the specific needs of migrant ELs.	Ensure that school district EL programs include MEP educators in curriculum and assessment planning and dissemination of information.	Develop outcome measures and/ or incentives that foster innovation of programs to promote effective literacy development of migrant EL students.

(Continued)

Table 9.1 (Continued)

Recommendation Goal	Program	State	Federal
Curriculum, implementation, and program design should begin from an asset-based framework.	When developing academic intervention programs, center migrant students' perspectives and experiences. Resist implementation of off-the-shelf curricula and programs without special consideration of migrant student needs.	Evaluations of MEP programs should conduct holistic (e.g., portfolio) assessments of programs' curriculum and instruction to ensure that program content and instruction is specific to migrant students' needs.	Develop outcome measures and/or incentives that reward asset-based program-building and assessment.
Educational interventions and the educators implementing programs should be culturally proficient in the specific needs and experiences of migrant children.	Implement ongoing professional development learning opportunities and professional requirements so that growth in cultural proficiency among personnel is a program goal.	Facilitate resources and support professional development and learning communities for educators of migrant students. Establish teacher credential programs with cultural proficiency training requirements.	By way of measurable outcomes and dedicated budget line items, MEP can require that states and programs develop cultural proficiency professional programs, certificates, credentialing, and/or provide evidence that demonstrates growth in cultural proficiency.
Increase authentic collaboration with parents in service delivery and educational interventions.	Incorporate parents' needs and families' cultural assets when developing programs and curriculum. Involve parents in authentic evaluation of programs.	Ensure that school districts include parents in service delivery, intervention planning, dissemination of information, and assessment.	Develop outcome measures and/or incentives that reward parental input, involvement, and collaboration.

Recommendation Goal	Program	State	Federal
Access and preparation for higher education should be an explicit objective and goal of MEP.	Prepare students with writing and other academic skills for college. Assist students with college and financial aid information and applications. Assist with selection and application for college.	Seek partnerships with higher education systems to develop and implement pathway programs for migrant students.	Develop a service area dedicated to access and preparation for higher education, with outcome goals and measures. Implement MSIX identifier from PK through higher education on a national level to capture college enrollment.
Increase or implement integrated service delivery across different government agencies and programs.	Establish collaborations with local, federal, and state partner programs to assist in identifying migrant students and offering seamless referral and follow-up to services.	Facilitate collaboration and coordination of services with other service agencies and programs by convening relevant partners, sharing data across programs, and requiring that school districts facilitate collaboration between various federal program leaders.	Incentivize, by funding or measurable outcomes, collaboration with programs funded by agencies whose significant portion of the targeted group are migrant children and families.

accountability levels of MEP (state, local, program) can undertake to move recommendations forward. In this way, improvements to educational services for migrant farmworker children and their families can have a greater likelihood of success with vertical support.

Acronyms

ABCD	Agri-business Child Development Center
BEA	Bilingual Education Act
BETAC	Bilingual/ESL Technical Assistance Center
CAMP	College Assistance Migrant Program
CDE	California Department of Education
CFR	Code of Federal Regulations
CNA	Comprehensive Needs Assessment
COE	Certificate of Eligibility
DSA	District Service Agreement
EL	English Learner
ESL	English as a Second Language
ESSA	Every Student Succeeds Act
FAPE	Free Appropriate Public Education
FBP	Family Biliteracy Project
GPRA	Government Performance and Results Act
HEP	High School Equivalency Program
IASA	Improving America's Schools Act
IDEA	Individuals with Disabilities Education
ID&R	Identification and Recruitment
IHE	Institutions of Higher Education
ILP	Individual Learning Plan
LEA	Local Educational Agency
LEP	Limited English Proficient
LTEL	Long Term English Learner
MEO	Migrant Education Office
MEP	Migrant Education Program
MSA	Migrant Summer Academies
MSHS	Migrant and Seasonal Head Start
MSIN	Migrant Student Information Network
MSIX	Migrant Student Records Exchange Initiative
MSLI	Migrant Student Leadership Institute
NCLB	No Child Left Behind
NFJP	National Farmworker Jobs Program

128 Acronyms

NPC	National PASS Center
OELA	Office of English Language Acquisition
OSEP	Office of Special Education Programs
OSY	Out-of-School Youth
PASS	Portable Assisted Study Sequence
RA	Regional Application
SEA	State Educational Agency
SPAC	State Parent Advisory Council
SSDP	State Services Delivery Plan
WIOA	Workforce Innovation and Opportunity Act

Contributors

Rodolfo Acosta, Ph.D., is an educational researcher in Southern California. His research sits at the intersection of K-12 policy, parent engagement, and equity of educational resources for historically underrepresented populations. Recent projects include a comprehensive needs assessment of the Migrant Education Program in San Diego, a multi-site mixed-methods evaluation of Supplementary Educational Services, and an ethnographic study of parents working to implement the Parent Empowerment Law in South Los Angeles.

Cristina Alfaro, Ph.D., is an Associate Professor and Department Chair, Dual Language and English Learner Education at San Diego State University. Her migrant family background as well as her experience as an elementary bilingual teacher and school administrator have served her well in preparing critically conscious bilingual teachers. As a teacher researcher, she has examined and published on the role of teachers' pedagogical and ideological clarity related to teaching practices for culturally and linguistically diverse students in low status communities.

Karen Cadiero-Kaplan, Ph.D., is a Professor of Dual Language and English Learner Education at San Diego State University. She is a researcher and social justice educator, and recently served the California Department of Education as the Director of the English Learner Support Division (2012–2014), leading state and federal programs for English Learner and Migrant Education.

Ann Cranston-Gingras, Ph.D., is a Professor of special education, Associate Dean for Graduate Education, and director of the Center for Migrant Education at the University of South Florida. Her research focuses on the educational needs of youth who have been marginalized by schools and society.

Alejandro González, Ed.D., manages and coordinates the Migrant Education Program in Orange County, California. His research areas include exploration of partnerships between the migrant community and educational institutions, parent engagement in the educational system, and migrant students' pathways to higher education.

130 *Contributors*

Ebelia Hernández, Ph.D., is an Associate Professor in the Graduate School of Education at Rutgers University. Dr. Hernández's research agenda centers on the Latino college student experience. She is particularly interested in how their experiences and the ways that they get involved may influence their holistic development.

Sera Hernandez, Ph.D., is an Assistant Professor of Dual Language and English Learner Education at San Diego State University. Her research focuses on the impact of state and federal language and education policies on language and literacy practices in schools, homes, and communities across California. She has worked in public K-12 schools and universities across the state for over 15 years.

Juan Felipe Herrera, MFA, was named U.S. Poet Laureate in 2015. Herrera is a poet, artist, and activist whose work is heavily influenced by his experience as the child of migrant farmworkers. He is the Tomás Rivera Endowed Chair at the University of California, Riverside.

Pablo Jasis, Ph.D., is an Associate Professor of Education at California State University, Fullerton, and is also the Principal Investigator of the High School Equivalency Program funded by the Office of Migrant Education and Chair of the Inclusive Education Task Force. His research areas include the relationship between communities and schools, bilingual and migrant education, and the empowerment of immigrant communities.

Sandra Kofford, Ed.D., has extensive experience working with at-risk and migrant students as a teacher, counselor, and high school administrator. Presently, as the Imperial County Migrant Education Program director, Dr. Kofford has been able to develop supplementary academic services that value migrant students' culture, language, and life experiences, by creating programs that positively connect migrant students with school, community, and higher education academic opportunities.

Randall B. Lindsey, Ph.D., is Emeritus Professor at California State University, Los Angeles. His research and publications are on Cultural Proficiency. Recent publications include *Culturally Proficient Practice: Supporting Educators of English Learning Students* (2012) and *A Culturally Proficient Response to the Common Core: Ensuring Equity through Professional Learning* (2015).

Anne-Marie Núñez, Ph.D., is an Associate Professor in the Educational Studies Department at The Ohio State University. Her research focuses on how to promote equity in postsecondary access and success, particularly for members of historically underserved groups, including Latino and migrant students.

Patricia A. Pérez, Ph.D., is a Professor at California State University, Fullerton. Her research focuses on postsecondary equity and equality of opportunity for Latina/o and im/migrant students. Dr. Pérez served as a co-principal investigator for a comprehensive needs assessment of the Migrant Education Program through the San Diego County Office of Education. Dr. Pérez is the co-editor of *Higher Education Access and Choice for Latino Students: Critical Findings and Theoretical Perspectives* published by Routledge. [Editor]

Reyes L. Quezada, Ph.D., is a Professor at the University of San Diego. His research focuses on cultural proficiency, equity, family-school and community engagement, and international education. He has published books and edited special issues in the *Journal of Multicultural Education*, the *Catholic Education Journal*, *Teaching Education*, and *Teacher Education Quarterly*.

Georgina Rivera-Singletary, Ph.D., is an education specialist supporting school transformation for Florida and the Islands Comprehensive Center. She holds a doctorate in curriculum and instruction/special education and has worked on behalf of migrant students as a teacher, school administrator, and district administrator for the second largest migrant program in Florida.

Fernando Rodríguez-Valls, Ph.D., is an Associate Professor in the Secondary Education Department at California State University, Fullerton. He has created partnerships with school districts, local educational agencies, and universities to develop and implement community-based [bi]literacy programs. Dr. Rodríguez-Valls' work focuses on equitable instructional practices for second language learners and migrant students as well as on the socio-cultural factors affecting their academic achievement, educational continuity, and school engagement.

Maria Estela Zarate, Ph.D., is a Professor of Educational Leadership at California State University, Fullerton. Her research explores factors that lead to successful high school completion and college enrollment for Latino students, with special attention to the experiences of English Language Learners. Recent projects include a comprehensive needs assessment with the Migrant Education Program in San Diego and the professional development of teachers to incorporate early college knowledge in content instruction. [Editor]

Index

Note: Page numbers in italics indicate figures.

after-school supplemental programs 35,
  43, 74–6
Agri-Business Child Development
  Centers (ABCD) 26
agricultural industry: and educational
  achievement 5–6; and immigration
  6–8; seasonal labor force in 8
anonymization 35, 68–9, 122
anti-affirmative action policies 86, 89
anti-migrant policies 82, 85, 89
aspirational capital 102
assessment tools 76–7
Association of Farmworker
  Opportunity Programs (AFOP) 6

Bellah, Robert 61
Bilingual Education Act (BEA) 18
bilingual education programs 16, 26,
  82, 86, 89
Bilingual/ESL Technical Assistance
  Center (BETAC) 26
Bode, Patty 39
Boise State University 24
Bracero Program 7, 117
BUENO Center for Multicultural
  Education (University of Colorado,
  Boulder) 26

California Department of Education
  (CDE) 67, 69, 77, 95, 97–8, 100
California Standards Test (CST) 4, 98
Center for Migrant Education (USF)
  26–7
Center for Multicultural and
  Educational Opportunities (Boise
  State University) 24
Cisneros, Sandra 74

collaboration: interagency 18–20, 27,
  63; parent-teacher 59, 62–3
college and university *see* postsecondary
  education
College Assistance Migrant Program
  (CAMP) 10, 21–4
college outreach programs 82, 86–92,
  122
Common Core State Standards (CCSS) 9
communication 62–3
community: challenges of 62–3;
  defining 56; strengths of 62–3
community of memory 61
Comprehensive Needs Assessment
  (CNA) 70–1, 100
Cornell University Community and
  Regional Development Institute 25
critical hope 102, 104, 106
cuentos (storytelling) 113–20
cultural capital 107
cultural proficiency: assessing 38;
  continuum of 36, 38, 45; of
  educators 34–47, 71, 106–8, 122;
  institutionalizing 46; tools of 36–8
Cultural Proficiency Continuum 36,
  38, 45
cultural tags 75–6
cultural wealth 96, 102–4, 106–9
culture of poverty approach 50
curriculum: collaboration in 3, 9;
  college preparatory 10; culturally
  relevant 35, 45, 69, 74, 106;
  disparities in 3, 16, 100, 102;
  diversity in 40; interdisciplinary
  76; recommendations for 123–5;
  student-centered 36; summer
  program 101

134 *Index*

deconstruction 75
deficit views 91
deportation 105
Derrida, Jacques 75
digital collages 75
District Service Agreement (DSA) 67–8,
71–2, 78
diversity: adapting to 45; curricular 40; of
migrant farmworkers 52; value of 40
DOE *see* U.S. Department of Education
DREAM Act 89
dropout rates 6
Dzogchen Ponlop, Rinpoche 78

early childhood education programs:
access to 4; comprehensive 24, 72;
parent-student involvement 73;
school readiness 3
education reform 103
educators: and advocacy 105–7, 123;
assumptions of 85, 88; and cultural
proficiency 34–47, 71, 106–8,
122; and diversity 45; equitable
partnerships 42; goal-linked
partnerships 41–2; ideological clarity
104, 106–7; linguistic knowledge
42; and parental involvement 53–4,
59, 61–2; partnerships with parents
104–5; as professional community
learners 47
Elementary and Secondary Education
Act (ESEA) 2, 7, 14–15
empowerment 51, 75
English language: and migrant
farmworker students 32–3;
proficiency in 4, 7
English Language Acquisition Program
17–18
English Language Arts (ELA) 9
English Language Learners (ELL):
challenges of 94; and educational
attainment 4; enrollment of 32–3;
funding for 18; and language
development 17; and native language
72–3; programs for 72, 78, 98
equitable partnerships 42
ESCORT (State University of New York
at Oneonta) 26
ESEA *see* Elementary and Secondary
Education Act (ESEA)
Every Student Succeeds Act (ESSA) 2,
15–16, 45, 97
experiential context 85

FAFSA 89
familial capital 102
Family Biliteracy Project (FBP) 35–6,
72–4, 76–8, 122
family literacy programs 72
Farmworker Program (Cornell
University) 25
"Farm Workers in California" 33
Federal Government Performance and
Results Act (GPRA) 100
financial aid 89–90
formative assessment 76
Free Appropriate Public Education
(FAPE) 19–20
Freire, Paulo 53, 60, 75
Fresh Fruit, Broken Bodies (Holmes) 43
funds of knowledge 45, 71, 104, 106

Geneseo Migrant Center 20–1
Gifted and Talented education (GATE)
115–16
goal-linked partnerships 41–2
Graffiti Wall 75
grammar of democracy 53, 60
Great Society Initiative 15
guest worker programs 7
Gutiérrez, Kris 86

Harvest of Shame 15
Head Start 24, 118
health-centered programs 67
high school: completion rates 6, 20–1,
67; equivalency programs 21–2;
portable study courses 20–1
High School Equivalency Program
(HEP) 10, 21–4
historicity 85, 89
Holmes, M. S. 43
Howard, T. C. 75

Idaho Department of Education 74
IDEA *see* Individuals with Disabilities
Education Act (IDEA)
identity: deconstructing 75; and
intersectionality 82–3, 89; migrant
75, 82–4; undocumented status 84
ideological clarity 104, 106–7
immigrants 98, 118
immigration: and economy 7–8;
and educational achievement 6–7;
Latina/o 6–7
inclusion programs 40
Individual Learning Plans 46, 68, 71

Index 135

Individuals with Disabilities Education Act (IDEA) 19–20, 121
inequality 72
intellectual commutes 74–5
intersectionality: and historicity 85, 89; and identity 82–4, 89; and postsecondary education 83; and social context 83–5
intersubjective context 85

Johnson, Lyndon B. 15

Language Explorers 74–8, 122
language skills: and inequality 72; parent-student involvement 73, 76; programs for 67, 71–4; and social justice 73; and writing 90
Latina/o students: challenges of 103–4; *cuentos* (storytelling) 113, 120; cultural wealth of 102–3; identity 75, 82–4; media representation 84; and nativism 86; and preschool programs 4
leadership roles 41, 60
learning disabilities 19–20
linguistic capital 102, 105
listening skills 74
literacy programs 72–6
local education agencies (LEA) 70; and data 2; and funding 16, 21, 69, 97–8, 101; and migrant farmworker students 9
Long Term English Learners (LTEL) 73

Macedo, D. 75
mathematics: national standards in 9; proficiency in 4
media representation 84
MEP *see* Migrant Education Program (MEP)
Mexico-California border 95–6, 104
Michigan State University 25
Mid-Hudson Migrant Outreach Center (SUNY-New Paltz) 25–6
Migrant and Seasonal Head Start Program (MSHS) 24
migrant education: accountability 99–102; assessing 76–7; best practices 72–7; collaboration in 18–20, 27; co-production 60–1; and cultural wealth 102–4, 106–9; deportation fears 105; and diversity 40–1, 45; effective 69, 71, 78;

evaluation of 70; federal initiatives 15–28, 97–101, 121; goals of 78; inclusion programs 40; policy enactment 95–7, 101; program development 41, 69–71, 78; recommendations for 123–5; research in 28; value of 5, 15, 55, 59; whole student approach to 108–9 *see also* Migrant Education Program (MEP)
Migrant Education Office (MEO) 67, 69, 73–4, 77
Migrant Education Program (MEP): accountability 99–102; and advocacy 56, 62, 108–9; and assessment 63; and communication 62–3; criteria for 8–9; effective 43–4; elements of 69; eligibility for 17, 99; as a family program 71–2; funding 2–3, 67, 97–9, 101; goals of 10, 101–2; health-centered programs 5; institutionalizing cultural knowledge 46; and mobility 1, 8–9; and out-of-school youth 6; participation in 1, 57–8; policy enactment 103, 121; portable study courses 21; postsecondary education 10; preschool programs 3–4; Priority for Services (PFS) children 39; provider-recipient model of 51; purpose of 3, 14–16, 51; recommendations for 123–5; services of 16, 96, 98–9
Migrant Even Start 72
migrant farmworker families: characteristics of 33; contributions of 51–2, 71; diversity of 52; and early childhood services 24; as education advocates 15, 55, 59–63, 119, 122; equitable partnerships 42; and exclusion 89; goal-linked partnerships 41–2; as guest workers 7, 117; and health 5; leadership roles for 41, 60; literacy programs 72–6; mobilization of 50, 53; narratives of 113–20; parent activism 53, 56–62; parental involvement 5, 53–5, 67; partnerships with teachers 59, 104–5; and poverty 5, 24, 33, 52, 72; social capital 68; strength and solidarity of 61; and struggle 58, 117–18; working conditions of 52
migrant farmworker students: abilities of 71–2; agency of 85, 87; assessing

136 Index

63; challenges of 2, 4–5, 14–15, 32–3, 52–4, 68, 94, 103–4; college outreach programs 82; and Common Core State Standards (CCSS) 9; cultural wealth of 102–3; deficit views 91; differences in 42–4; and educational achievement 4–6; and education services 24–8, 50–1, 122–3; and empowerment 51, 75; and English language acquisition 4, 7, 17–19, 26, 33, 72–4; enrollment of 34; expectations for 85; experiential context 85; grant programs for 21–3; health-centered programs 67; high school completion rates of 6, 20–1; identity 75, 82–4, 86, 89; lack of belonging 119, 122; and language/learning disabilities 19–20; language skills 67, 72–6; marginalization of 35–6, 68–9, 82, 86, 90–1, 94; and mathematics 4; media representation 84; mobility of 2, 5–6, 8–9, 19, 32, 39, 43, 52, 68, 94, 108; needs of 68; portable study courses 20–1; and postsecondary education 10–11, 22–7, 82–92, 94–5, 118, 122; and poverty 2, 6, 19, 52–3, 82; and preschool programs 3–4; and qualifying moves 17; and social context 83–5, 89; and stress 105–6; supporting 1, 3, 33–4; systematic oppression of 77

Migrant Health (SUNY-New Paltz) 26
Migrant Health Program 5
Migrant Student Information Network (MSIN) 69
Migrant Student Leadership Institute (MSLI) 10, 86–9, 91
Migrant Student Records Exchange Initiative (MSIX) 69
Migrant Student Services Center (Michigan State University) 25
Migrant Summer Academies 35–6
Migrant Summer Leadership Institute (MSLI) 77
Mini-Corps 95
Mixteco language 42, 67, 73
mobility see residential mobility
monolingualism 72–3
multicultural education 26; approaches to 32; and cultural proficiency 35; and migrant families 73; and migrant

farmworker students 16; promotion of 71; research on 26
multilingual education 71, 73
multimodal stories 74–5
Murrow, Edward R. 15

Nahuatl language 67
National Farmworker Jobs Program (NFJP) 23–4
National Migrant Education hotline 26
National PASS Center (NPC) 21
nativism 86
Navarrette, Ruben 113
navigational capital 102, 105
Network of Experts in Social Sciences of Education and training (NESSE) 68
Newman, S. 75
Nieto, Sonia 39, 77
No Child Left Behind Act 15, 18
Norris, C. 75
North American Free Trade Agreement (NAFTA) 7

Obama, Barack 15
Office of English Language Acquisition (OELA) 17–18
Office of Migrant Education (OME) 3, 16, 21–2, 43, 69, 72, 95–6, 100
Office of Special Education Programs (OSEP) 20
organizational context 83
Osterling, J. 55
Out-of-School Youth program 6, 67, 99

parent action committees (PAC) 5
parent activism 53, 56–62
Parent Advisory Councils 42
parental involvement: partnerships for 54–5; perceptions of 53–4; programs for 67; teacher collaboration 59
pedagogy of solidarity 60
Portable Assisted Study Sequence program (PASS) 20–1
portfolios 76
postsecondary education: access to 83, 86–92; barriers to 10–11, 83–6, 94–5; grant programs for 21–3; and migrant farmworker students 10–11, 21–7, 82–3, 118, 122; outreach programs 82

Index   137

poverty: federal initiatives 50; and migrant families 5, 24, 33, 52, 72; and migrant farmworker students 2, 6, 19, 52–3, 82
preschool programs: enrollment in 4; and school readiness 3 *see also* early childhood education programs
Priority for Services (PFS) children 39
professional community learners 47

qualifying moves 8–9, 17

Regional Applications (RA) 67–8, 71–2, 78
Rendón, Laura 113
representational context 83–5, 89
residential mobility: and educational achievement 8–9; and seasonal labor force 8
resistance capital 102
Rodriguez, Richard 113

school readiness: and preschool programs 3; programs for 67
SEA *see* State Educational Agencies (SEA)
service model 51
Shakur, Tupac 74
social capital 68, 102
social contexts: experiential 85; intersubjective 85; organizational 83; representational 83–5, 89
social justice 38–40, 73
sociocritical literacy 87–9
Soto, Gary 74
Spanish language 7, 67, 73, 105
speaking skills 74
Speech and Debate Program 77
State Educational Agencies (SEA) 2, 69–70, 97–8, 101

State Parent Advisory Council (SPAC) 69
State Service Delivery Plan (SSDP) 69–71, 73, 100–1
State University of New York at New Paltz 25–6
State University of New York at Oneonta 26

teachers *see* educators
testimonios approach 55–6, 96, 104
Title 1 15, 67, 97–8, 101, 103, 121
Title 1. Part C 103, 121
Title III Language Instruction for English Learners and Immigrant Students 18, 97–8, 101, 103, 121
Tools of Cultural Proficiency 36–8
transnational migration 33
Triqui language 42, 67, 73

underserved communities: and education 51; and financial aid 90; mobilization of 53
undocumented status 84, 91
United Farm Workers 85
University of Colorado, Boulder 26
University of South Florida Center for Migrant Education 26–7
U.S. Department of Education (DOE) 3, 21, 72, 97

Workforce Innovation and Opportunity Act (WIOA) 23
writing skills 74, 87–8, 90, 122

Xinca language 105

Yang, Gene Luen 74
Yosso, T. J. 96, 102, 104, 108

Zapoteco language 42, 67, 73